THE
SCIEN
CHEF
TRAVELS AROUND
THE WORLD

THE SCIENCE CHEF
TRAVELS AROUND THE WORLD

Fun Food Experiments and Recipes for Kids

Joan D'Amico

Karen Eich Drummond, R.D.

Illustrations by Tina Cash-Walsh

John Wiley & Sons, Inc.

New York • Chichester • Brisbane • Toronto • Singapore

This text is printed on acid-free paper.

R01035 19300

The publisher and the author have made every reasonable effort to ensure that the experiments and activities in the book are safe when conducted as instructed but assume no responsibility for any damage caused or sustained while performing the experiments or activities in this book. Parents, guardians, and/or teachers should supervise young readers who undertake the experiments and activities in this book.

Library of Congress Cataloging-in-Publication Data
D'Amico, Joan
    The science chef travels around the world : fun food experiments
and recipes for kids / Joan D'Amico, Karen Eich Drummond ;
illustrations by Tina Cash-Walsh
        p. cm.
    Includes index.
    Summary: Introduces fourteen countries, including Canada, Mexico, and Brazil, describes an experiment related to some basic food ingredient typical for each country, and provides a recipe for a complete meal based on each food.
    ISBN 0–471–11779–X (pbk. : alk. paper)
    1. Cookery—Juvenile literature. 2. Science—Experiments—Juvenile literature.
3. Cookery, International—Juvenile literature. 4. Food—Juvenile literature.
[1. Food. 2. Cookery. 3. Science—Experiments. 4. Experiments.]
I. Drummond, Karen Eich. II. Cash-Walsh, Tina, ill. III. Title.
TX652.5.D35   1996
641.5—dc20   95-32952

Printed in the United States of America
10 9 8 7 6 5 4 3 2 1

Dedicated to all the world's children.

CONTENTS

ABOUT THIS BOOK

Our first book, *The Science Chef,* taught you about science in new and tasty ways. In this book, *The Science Chef Travels Around the World,* not only will you learn the science of cooking, you'll also go on exciting journeys to foreign lands, where you'll learn about new foods, prepare international dishes, and see how people from other cultures eat. You probably know that chopsticks are used to eat food in China, but did you know that in India people use pieces of bread or rice to scoop food off their plates?

In this book you'll get to travel to fourteen different countries, including China and India. But before you begin your journey, be sure to look at the section called "Discovering the Kitchen," which covers the basics about kitchen tools, cooking skills, and safety rules. Read it carefully before doing any of the experiments or trying any of the recipes.

Once you've read "Discovering the Kitchen," you'll be ready to begin your trip. You'll learn to prepare authentic meals of each country you visit. The first destination is North America, where you'll travel to Canada. From there you'll go south of the U.S. border to visit Mexico, and then travel to Brazil, the largest country in South America. From South America you'll voyage across the Atlantic to Europe, where you'll visit Italy, France, Germany, and Spain. After Europe, you'll touch down in Israel, which is in the Middle East, then you'll go onward to Asia. In Asia, you'll visit India, China, Japan, and Thailand. But your trip isn't over yet! Before you head home, you'll visit Morocco and Ghana in Africa, where human life began.

Each chapter begins with an explanation of the foods and meals of that country. Then you'll explore different science topics with an experiment you can do right in your kitchen, followed by an easy-to-make recipe that often uses the food from the experiment. Altogether there are over 50 experiments and international recipes for you to try. Each experiment includes a purpose statement, a list of the materials you'll need, the steps to follow, and an explanation of what happened and why. None of the experiments requires any previous cooking experience.

After doing the experiment, you can have some fun preparing a meal typical of the country you are visiting. For example, in Italy, you'll dry tomatoes; then, you'll make an Italian meal of focaccia topped with dried tomatoes, an antipasto salad, and cannoli for dessert.

Each recipe is rated according to how much cooking experience is required. The easiest recipes, marked with one chef's hat (called a toque), require no previous cooking experience. Intermediate recipes, with two chefs' hats, require some cooking experience. "Pro" recipes, with three chefs' hats, require more advanced cooking skills.

easiest

intermediate

pro

Always be sure you have an adult to guide you when the experiment or recipe asks you to use the oven, the stove, electrical appliances, or a sharp knife.

These recipes also

- list the time you will need to make them, the kitchen tools you'll need, and the number of servings each recipe makes;
- use easy-to-find ingredients and standard kitchen equipment;
- give metric equivalents for all ingredients;
- are kid-tested and kid-approved; and
- emphasize wholesome ingredients.

At the end of the book you'll find a glossary and sections on nutrition and food safety, including an explanation of how to read a food label and a chart listing the nutritional values of all the recipes in the book.

So put on your apron, wash your hands, roll up your sleeves, and get ready to become an international Science Chef. We hope you have as much fun learning, cooking, and eating as we did writing this book for you!

Joan D'Amico
Wayne, New Jersey

Karen Eich Drummond
Yardley, Pennsylvania

DISCOVERING THE KITCHEN

THE SCIENCE CHEF'S TOOLS OF THE TRADE

colander

baking pan

cutting board

biscuit cutter

blender

grater

cookie sheet

electric mixer

Let's take a close look at the cooking equipment in your kitchen. These are the basic tools you'll need to do the experiments and prepare the recipes in this book. Any kitchen tools that are used in only one or two recipes are described within those recipes.

baking pan   A square or rectangular pan used for baking and cooking foods in the oven. The most common sizes are 9-by-13-inch (13.5-by-32.5-cm) and 8-inch (20-cm) square.

biscuit cutter   A round outline, usually made from metal, used to cut biscuits from dough.

blender   A glass or plastic cylinder with a rotating blade at the bottom. The blender has different speeds and is used for mixing, blending, grinding, and pureeing.

colander   A large perforated bowl used for rinsing food and draining pasta or other foods.

cookie sheet   A large rectangular pan with no sides or with half-inch (1.2 cm) sides, used for baking cookies and other foods.

cutting board   Made from wood or plastic, cutting boards provide a surface on which to cut foods.

electric mixer   Two beaters that rotate to mix ingredients together. Used for mashed potatoes, cake batters, and other mixing jobs.

grater   Used for shredding and grating foods such as vegetables and cheese.

knives:

- **paring knife**   A knife with a small pointed blade used for trimming and paring vegetables and fruits and other cutting jobs that don't require a larger knife. (Most recipes in this book call for a knife. You will find the paring knife works well in most situations.)

- **peeler**   A handheld tool that removes the peel from fruits and vegetables.

- **sandwich spreader**   A knife with a dull blade that is designed to spread fillings on bread.

- **table knife**   A knife used as a utensil at the table.

paring knife

sandwich spreader

layer cake pans   Round metal pans used to bake layers of a cake.

layer cake pan

loaf pan   A rectangular metal or glass pan with slanted sides. Used in both baking (for breads, for example) and cooking (for meat loaf, for example).

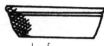

loaf pan

measuring cups   Cups with measurements (½ cup, ⅓ cup, etc.) on the sides and spouts for easy pouring.

measuring cup

measuring spoons   Used for measuring small amounts of foods such as spices. They come in a set of 1 tablespoon, 1 teaspoon, ½ teaspoon, and ¼ teaspoon.

measuring spoons

microwave dish   A dish that can safely be used in the microwave oven. The best microwave dishes say "microwave safe" on the label. Don't use metal pans, aluminum foil, plastic foam containers, brown paper bags, plastic wrap, or margarine tubs in the microwave.

mixing bowls   Round-bottomed bowls used for mixing and whipping all kinds of foods.

muffin tins   Metal or glass pans with small, round cups used for baking muffins and cupcakes.

microwave dish

muffin tin

pans:

- **frying pan** (also called a skillet or a sauté pan) Used for cooking foods, such as hamburgers or onions, in hot fat.

frying pan

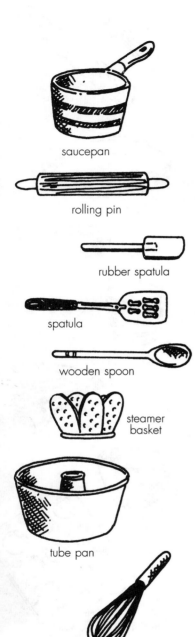

saucepan

rolling pin

rubber spatula

spatula

wooden spoon

steamer basket

tube pan

wire whip

- **griddle**   A flat surface without sides used for cooking pancakes, French toast, and bacon.
- **saucepan** (also called a pot)   Used for general stovetop cooking, such as boiling pasta or simmering a sauce.

pastry blender   A curved metal tool used for cutting fats into flour.

rolling pin   A wooden or plastic roller used to flatten items such as pie crust and biscuit dough.

rubber spatula   A flexible rubber or plastic tip on a long handle. It is used to scrape bowls, pots, and pans and for **folding** (a gentle over-and-under motion) ingredients into whipped cream or other whipped batter.

spatula   A flat metal or plastic tool used for lifting and turning meats, eggs, and other foods.

spoons:

- **teaspoon**   A spoon used for measuring. Also the name for the spoon normally used as a utensil at the table.
- **wooden spoon**   Used for mixing ingredients together and stirring.

steamer basket   A perforated metal basket used to hold vegetables or other foods so that they can be steamed in a saucepan.

tube pan   A metal cake pan with a center tube used for making angel food cakes, bundt cakes, and special breads.

wire whip   Used especially for whipping egg whites and cream.

wire rack   Used for cooling baked goods.

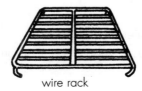

wire rack

COOKING SKILLS

Chefs need to master cutting and measuring skills and the basics of mixing and stovetop cooking. Here are the skills you will be practicing as you try the recipes in this book.

CUTTING

Foods are cut before cooking so that they will look good and cook evenly. Place the food to be cut on a cutting board and use a knife that is a comfortable size for your hand. To hold the knife, place your hand on top of the handle and fit your fingers around the handle. The grip should be secure but relaxed. In your other hand, hold the item being cut. Keep your fingertips curled under to protect them from cuts. (See the "Safety Rules" section of this chapter for more on how to cut safely.)

Here are some commonly used cutting terms you'll need to know.

chop To cut into irregularly shaped pieces.

dice To cut into cubes of the same size.

mince To chop very fine.

slice To cut into uniform slices.

Grating and shredding are also examples of cutting.

grate To rub a food across a grater's tiny punched holes to produce small or fine pieces of food. Hard cheeses and some vegetables are grated.

shred To rub a food across a surface with medium to large holes or slits. Shredded foods look like strips. The cheese used for making pizza is always shredded.

chopped

diced

sliced

minced

grate

shred

MEASURING

Ingredients can be measured in three different ways: by counting (six apples), by measuring volume (½ cup of applesauce), or by measuring weight (a pound of apples).

To measure the volume of a liquid, always place the measuring cup on a flat surface and check that the liquid goes up to the proper line on the measuring cup while looking directly at it at eye level.

To measure the volume of a dry ingredient, such as flour, spoon it into the measuring cup and level it off with a table knife. Do not pack the cup with the dry ingredient—that is, don't press down on it to make room for more—unless the recipe says to.

The United States is the only major country that uses the English system of measures. By this system, weight is measured in pounds; volume in gallons, quarts, cups, and fluid ounces; and length in feet and inches. Most other countries use a simpler system of measures called the metric system. Both types of measurements are given for all ingredients used in this book.

In the metric system, there is one basic unit for each type of measurement:

The *gram* (g) is the basic unit of weight.

The *liter* (L) is the basic unit of volume.

The *meter* (m) is the basic unit of length.

The *degree Celsius* (°C) is the basic unit of temperature.

The metric system is a decimal-based system of measures, meaning that units for a given quantity are related by factors of 10. For example a kilogram is 1,000 grams, while a milligram is ⅟₁₀₀₀ gram.

The chart shows the metric abbreviations and equivalents used in this book.

English–Metric Equivalents

Weight

2.2 pounds = 1 kilogram (kg)

1 pound = 454 grams (g)

1 ounce = 28.35 grams (g)

Volume

33.8 fluid ounces = 1 liter (L)

1 quart = 946 milliliters (ml)
    = 1 liter (L)

1 cup = 240 milliliters (ml)

1 fluid ounce = 30 milliliters (ml)

1 tablespoon = 15 milliliters (ml)

1 teaspoon = 5 milliliters (ml)

Length

1 inch = 2.54 centimeters (cm)
    or 25 millimeters (mm)

Temperature

To convert degrees Fahrenheit (°F) to degrees Celsius (°C), subtract 32, then divide by 9 and multiply by 5.

MIXING

There are all kinds of mixing! Here are definitions of the most common types.

beat   To move a utensil back and forth to blend ingredients together.

cream   To mix a solid fat (usually margarine or butter) and sugar by pressing them against a bowl with the back of a spoon until they look creamy.

cut in   To combine a fat with a flour using a cutting motion until the mixture is in the shape of peas.

fold   To move a utensil with a gentle over-and-under motion.

mix   To combine ingredients so that they are all evenly distributed.

toss   To mix ingredients lightly until they are well coated with a dressing or well blended.

whip   To beat rapidly using a circular motion, usually with a wire whip, to incorporate air into the mixture (such as in making whipped cream).

whisk   To beat ingredients together lightly with a wire whip until they are well blended.

beat

fold

whip

STOVETOP COOKING

There are different ways to cook on your stove. Here are descriptions of cooking methods you will be practicing as you try the recipes in this book. Because it is easy to get burned while cooking on the stove, see the "Safety Rules" section of this chapter.

boil   To heat a liquid to its boiling point, or to cook in a boiling liquid. Water boils at 212°F (100°C). You can tell it is boiling when you see lots of large bubbles popping on the surface. When a liquid boils, it is turning into water vapor (the gas state of water). What is called "steam" is the

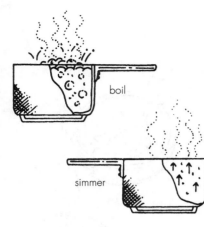

boil

simmer

sauté

cooled vapor returning to the liquid state of water. Water can't get any hotter than 212°F (100°C); it can only make water vapor faster. Boiling is most often used for cooking pasta.

simmer   To heat a liquid to just below its boiling point, or to cook in a simmering liquid. You can tell a liquid is simmering when it has bubbles floating slowly to the surface. Most foods cooked in liquid are simmered. Always watch simmering foods closely so that they do not boil.

steam   To cook in steam. Steam has much more heat and cooks foods more quickly than boiling water does. Steaming is an excellent method for cooking most vegetables.

panfry   To cook in a pan over moderate heat in a small amount of fat. Hamburgers are an example of a food that can be panfried.

stir-fry   To cook bite-sized pieces of food over medium-high heat in a small amount of oil while stirring constantly. Stir-frying is the most common method of cooking Chinese food.

sauté   To cook quickly in a pan over medium-high heat in a small amount of fat. Vegetables, especially onions, are often sautéed in oil to bring out their flavor and brown them.

CRACKING AND SEPARATING EGGS

It is best to crack an egg into a clear glass cup (such as a measuring cup) before adding it to the other ingredients. That way if the egg smells bad or has a red spot, you can throw it out before the egg goes in with the other ingredients. An egg with a red spot is safe to eat, but it is usually thrown out because of its appearance. You should also check for eggshells in the egg before adding the egg to the other ingredients.

Sometimes you will need to separate the egg yolk from the egg white for a recipe. To do this, crack the egg over an egg separator and a bowl. Make sure you get the yolk in the middle. The whites will drain out into the bowl. If you don't have an egg separator, you can separate an egg by cracking it over a bowl, keeping the yolk in one half of the shell. Carefully pass the egg yolk from one half of the shell to the other without letting it break until the whites have all fallen into the bowl.

KNEADING DOUGH

Kneading is the process of working dough into a smooth mass by pressing and folding. This develops the **gluten** (an elastic substance in flour that gives bread its sturdy texture) and mixes the ingredients. Kneading is important for the bread to have the right texture.

To knead, place the ball of dough in front of you on a lightly floured board or table. Press the dough out, then fold in half. Give the dough a quarter turn, then press, fold, and turn again. Continue kneading until the dough is smooth.

SAFETY RULES

The kitchen can be a safe, or a very dangerous, part of your home. What's dangerous in your kitchen? Sharp knives, boiling water, and hot oil are a few things. Always check with an adult before trying any of the recipes. Talk to him or her about what you are allowed to do by yourself and when you need an adult's assistance. And always follow these safety guidelines.

AROUND THE STOVE AND OVEN

- Get your parent's permission before using a stove or oven.
- Don't wear long, baggy shirts or sweaters when cooking. They could catch fire.
- Never turn your back on a frying pan that contains oil.
- Never fry with oil at a high temperature.
- Don't spray a pan with vegetable oil cooking spray over the stove or near heat. Oil will burn at high temperatures, so spray the pan over the sink.
- If a fire starts in a pan on the stove, you can smother it by covering it with the pan lid or pouring baking soda on it. Never use water to put out a fire in a pan with oil—it only makes a fire worse.
- Always use pot holders or wear oven mitts when using the oven or handling something that is hot. Make sure your pot holders are not wet. Wet pot holders transmit the heat from the hot item you are holding directly to your skin.

- Don't overfill pans with boiling or simmering liquids.
- Open pan lids away from you to let steam escape safely.
- Keep pan handles turned away from the edge of the stove. Knocking against them can splatter hot food.
- Stir foods with long-handled spoons.
- Keep pets and small children away from hot stoves and ovens during cooking. (Try to keep them out of the kitchen altogether.)

USING ANY APPLIANCE

- Use an appliance only if you know exactly how to operate it.
- Never operate an appliance that is near the sink or in water.
- Don't use frayed electrical cords or damaged plugs and outlets. Tell an adult.

USING A MICROWAVE OVEN

- Use only microwave-safe cookware, paper towels, paper plates, or paper cups.
- Use pot holders to remove items.
- If a dish is covered, make sure there is some opening through which steam can escape during cooking.
- When taking foods out of the microwave, open the container so that steam escapes *away* from your hands and face.
- To keep foods like potatoes and hot dogs from bursting, pierce them with a fork before putting them into the microwave.
- Never try to cook a whole egg in the microwave—it will burst!

USING A KNIFE

- Get your parent's permission before using any knife.
- Always pick up a knife by its handle.
- Pay attention to what you're doing!
- Cut away from the body and away from anyone near you.
- Use a sliding, back-and-forth motion when slicing foods with a knife.
- Don't leave a knife near the edge of a table. It can be easily knocked off, or a small child may touch it.
- Don't try to catch a falling knife.
- Don't walk with a knife in the blade-up position.
- Don't use knives to cut string, or to open cans or bottles, or as a screwdriver.
- Don't put a knife into a sink full of water. Instead, put it on the drainboard, to avoid cutting yourself.

PART 1

NORTH AMERICA

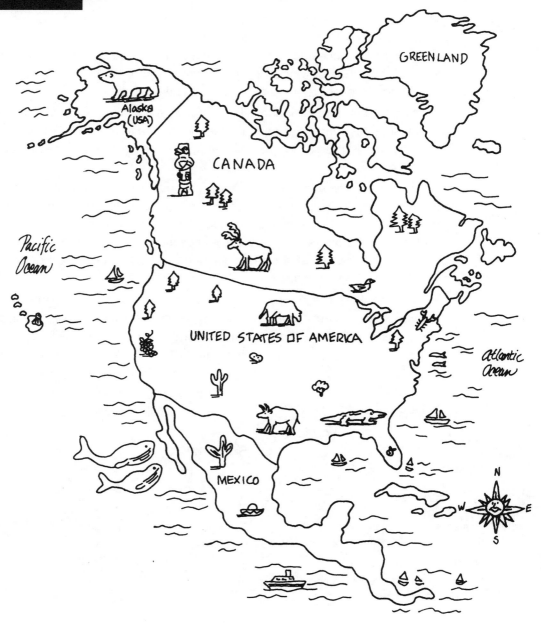

GREENLAND

Alaska (USA)

CANADA

Pacific Ocean

UNITED STATES OF AMERICA

Atlantic Ocean

MEXICO

N W E S

What country covers more land area than any other nation in North or South America? Canada! It sweeps from the Atlantic Ocean to the Pacific Ocean, and reaches up to the Arctic north. This huge country is divided into ten regions called provinces, plus two other regions called territories. As you can imagine, every region has its own favorite foods.

Seafood is popular in the Atlantic Provinces. Look for lobster, salmon, Digby scallops, and Malpeque oysters on the menu. For more familiar flavors, try freshly pressed apple cider, maple syrup with baked beans, or brown bread.

To experience something really new in the Atlantic province of New Brunswick, try fiddlehead ferns. Each spring, residents wander along stream banks to pick fresh green fiddleheads. Often, the fiddleheads are steamed and then made into soups, and sometimes they are marinated. Another unusual New Brunswick food is a sun-dried red seaweed called **dulse**, which is eaten as a snack.

In the Yukon Territory, next to Alaska, you'll discover lots of game–wild animals, fowl, or fish that are hunted for sport. Deer meat, called **venison**, is a popular game meat on Yukon menus. In the province of Alberta, where there are thousand-acre ranches, pit-cooked barbecues and steaks are more popular.

Throughout Canada, meals are quite similar to meals eaten in the United States. Breakfast and lunch

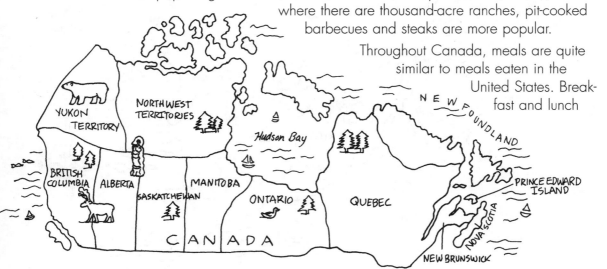

are smaller than dinner, which is the main meal of the day. A typical Canadian meal consists of a main dish of meat, poultry, or seafood; side dishes of vegetables and starches; and a salad. Try the following activity to learn more about the main ingredient in salads: lettuce.

WHAT KEEPS LETTUCE CRISP?

EXPERIMENT

Materials

2 large lettuce leaves
2 small bowls

Purpose

To determine what makes lettuce wilt.

Procedure

1. Put one of the lettuce leaves in one bowl.

2. Tear the other lettuce leaf into bite-sized pieces, and place it in the other bowl.

3. Let the bowls stand at room temperature for 1 hour.

4. After 1 hour, look at the lettuce in both bowls. Which bowl contains crisp lettuce? Which bowl contains wilted lettuce?

What Happened?

The torn lettuce is much more wilted than the whole leaf. This is because more water can escape from the many surfaces of torn leaves. Vegetables contain much water. In fact, lettuce is over 90 percent water! Water is what makes lettuce and other vegetables crisp and good to eat.

Put the wilted whole leaf in cold water for 5 to 10 minutes so that it will absorb some of the water and become crisp again! Use more lettuce leaves in the Southwestern Ontario Fruit Salad. Serve your fruit salad with the Open-Faced Barbecue Beef Sandwich and Maple Syrup Baked Beans for a complete Canadian meal!

Southwestern Ontario Fruit Salad

Time
15 minutes

Tools
knife
strawberry huller (optional)
cutting board
large bowl
serving dish

Makes
6 servings

During the warm months, fruits flourish in the southwestern area of Ontario province. This salad features many fruits.

Ingredients

1 cup (240 ml) fresh strawberries

2 apples

1 nectarine

1 plum

½ cup (120 ml) seedless grapes

½ cup (120 ml) orange juice

several whole lettuce leaves

½ cup (120 ml) shredded coconut

Steps

1. Wash all the fruits.

2. Remove the stems from the strawberries with a knife or strawberry huller.

3. Using a knife on a cutting board, cut the strawberries into bite-sized pieces.

4. Cut the apples, nectarine, and plum in quarters and remove their seeds and pits.

5. Slice the apples, nectarine, and plum.

6. Put the sliced fruit and the grapes in a large bowl.

7. Add the orange juice, then toss the fruit.

8. Put the lettuce leaves on the serving dish, then top them with the fruit.

9. Sprinkle coconut over the fruit and serve.

Orange juice prevents the apple slices from turning black.

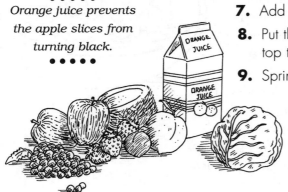

Open-Faced Barbecue Beef Sandwich

In the city of Calgary and throughout the province of Alberta, barbecued foods are popular. Calgary, located in the foothills of the Canadian Rockies, was the host of the 1988 Winter Olympics. It also hosts the Calgary Stampede, one of the world's best-known rodeos.

Time
15 minutes

Tools
large saucepan with lid

knife

broiler pan

serving dish

spoon

Makes
4 servings

Ingredients

1 cup (240 ml) your favorite barbecue sauce

¾ pound (340 g) thinly sliced cooked roast beef

4 French-style rolls

Steps

1. In a large saucepan, add just enough barbecue sauce to cover the bottom of the pan.

2. Lay the roast beef on top of the barbecue sauce.

3. Pour the rest of the barbecue sauce on top of the meat.

4. Set the heat to medium.

5. When the barbecue sauce starts to bubble, reduce the heat to low.

6. Cover the pan and simmer the meat for 5 minutes.

7. While the meat is simmering, preheat the broiler.

8. Split the rolls with a knife and put them on the broiler pan.

• • • • •
When broiling,
always keep an eye
on the food to prevent
overcooking or a fire.
• • • • •

9. Placing the broiler pan at least 4 inches (10 cm) from the heating element, toast the rolls for 1 to 2 minutes or until golden brown. Keep an eye on the rolls at all times to make sure they do not overcook!

10. Using oven mitts, remove the broiler pan. Transfer the toasted rolls to a serving dish. Spoon some of the cooked meat on top of each roll and serve immediately.

Maple Syrup Baked Beans

In the Atlantic Provinces, Canadians tap maple trees to get maple syrup. Maple syrup dinners are a tradition in many community churches. Jugs of maple syrup are served with pancakes, brown bread, baked beans, and other foods. Try making your own Maple Syrup Baked Beans.

Time
10 minutes to prepare
plus
40 minutes to bake

Tools
can opener

colander

small casserole dish

Makes
6 servings

Ingredients

16-ounce (454-g) can baked beans in tomato sauce

15½-ounce (439-g) can red kidney beans

2 tablespoons (30 ml) brown sugar

¼ cup (60 ml) maple-flavored pancake syrup

Steps

1. Preheat oven to 350°F (190°C).

2. Open both cans of beans.

3. Empty the can of red kidney beans into a colander to drain off the liquid.

4. Put both kinds of beans, the brown sugar, and pancake syrup in a small casserole dish and mix well.

5. Bake for 40 minutes.

What we call pancake syrup is a sugar syrup with maple flavoring. Real maple syrup is delicious, but very expensive.

CHAPTER 2
MEXICO

· ·

About 1519, when the Spanish explorer Hernando Cortés (1485–1547) landed in what is now known as Mexico, he discovered the civilization of the Aztecs. Cortés was introduced to many foods he had never seen before: tomatoes, corn, squash, beans, potatoes, chili peppers, turkey, chocolate, vanilla, cinnamon, pineapple, sweet potatoes, and much more. In turn, the Spanish explorers introduced the Aztecs to new foods such as wheat and rice. This blend of Spanish and Aztec foods resulted in what has become today's Mexican foods.

If you have ever eaten a taco or an enchilada, then you are already familiar with one staple of Mexican cooking: tortillas! **Tortillas** (tor-TEE-yahs) are thin, flat pancakes that are eaten as bread at most Mexican meals. They are often filled with meat, beans, and vegetables, then rolled or folded to hold the ingredients together. Many Mexicans buy fresh tortillas daily from a store called a **tortillería** (tor-tee-yah-REE-ah).

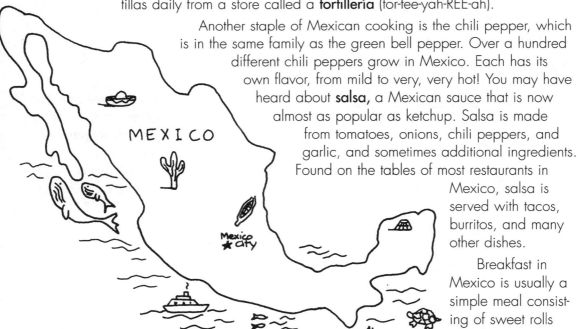

Another staple of Mexican cooking is the chili pepper, which is in the same family as the green bell pepper. Over a hundred different chili peppers grow in Mexico. Each has its own flavor, from mild to very, very hot! You may have heard about **salsa,** a Mexican sauce that is now almost as popular as ketchup. Salsa is made from tomatoes, onions, chili peppers, and garlic, and sometimes additional ingredients. Found on the tables of most restaurants in Mexico, salsa is served with tacos, burritos, and many other dishes.

Breakfast in Mexico is usually a simple meal consisting of sweet rolls and Mexican hot chocolate. Mexican hot chocolate uses a special type of chocolate that contains sugar and cinnamon, a sweet spice. The chocolate is whipped into a froth with a wooden beater called a **molinillo** (moh-lee-NEE-yoh).

In Mexico, the heaviest meal is eaten in the middle of the day. Lunch might include chicken rice soup, tortillas with chicken and vegetables, refried beans, and fresh fruit. Supper is lighter and may consist of bean salad, tortillas with salsa, and rice pudding for dessert.

Dry beans are often seen in Mexican dishes, such as chili con carne and refried beans. Do the following experiment with beans to learn how soaking dry beans can make them soft and tender.

HOW DOES SOAKING AFFECT DRIED BEANS?

EXPERIMENT

Materials
1 pound (454 g) dry kidney beans
colander
large bowl with cover
2 medium saucepans with lids
fork

Procedure
1. Wash the beans in a colander. Remove any damaged beans or foreign materials.
2. Put half of the beans in a large bowl. Fill the bowl about three quarters full with water. Cover the bowl and place it in the refrigerator overnight.
3. The next day, put the rest of the dry kidney beans in one of the saucepans, along with 1½ cups (360 ml) of water.

Purpose
To determine whether soaking beans affects their cooking time.

4. Remove the beans from the refrigerator. Using a colander, drain the beans and discard the water.

5. Place the presoaked, refrigerated beans and 1½ cups (360 ml) of water in the other saucepan.

6. Place both saucepans on burners, and set the heat to high.

7. Once the beans are boiling, reduce the heat to low and simmer, covered, until they are tender when pierced with a fork. Record the time it takes each pot of beans to soften.

What Happened?

The beans that were soaked overnight in water cooked much more quickly than the beans that were not presoaked. Dry beans have a hard outer skin, called the **seed coat**, which resists water. However, there is no seed coat at the **hilum**, the point where the seed was attached to the pod. Water can be absorbed into the bean only through the hilum. When beans are soaked in water, the **starches** (nutrients your body burns for energy) inside the bean absorb the water by a process called **gelatinization**. Beans actually double in size during soaking! Once soaked, beans cook faster, because they are full of water.

There is one more benefit to soaking beans. Soaking brings certain sugars out of dry beans. Many people cannot digest these sugars properly, so eating nonsoaked beans causes bloating and unpleasant gases. Throwing out the soaking water gets rid of many of the problem sugars.

Use the presoaked kidney beans in the Mexican Bean Salad recipe. Serve your salad with Sizzling Chicken Fajitas, Confetti Rice, and Fast 'n' Easy Cornbread, then top these off with Rice Pudding for an authentic Mexican meal!

Time
30 minutes

Tools
can opener

colander

medium bowl

knife

cutting board

wire whip

small bowl

plastic wrap

Makes
8 servings

• • • • •
Mexican Bean Salad
will keep in the refrigerator
for up to 7 days.
• • • • •

Mexicans enjoy a wide variety of beans,
such as navy beans and kidney beans.
This salad uses several Mexican favorites.

Ingredients

15½-oz. (439-g) can red kidney beans

14½-oz. (411-g) can green beans

14-oz. (397-g) can pinto beans

1 medium onion

2 celery stalks

⅓ cup (80 ml) vinegar

2 tablespoons (30 ml) olive oil

¼ teaspoon (2 ml) salt

⅛ teaspoon (1 ml) pepper

Steps

1. Open the cans of kidney beans, green beans, and pinto beans.

2. Empty all the cans into a colander to drain off the liquid.

3. Put the beans in a medium bowl.

4. Remove the outer, papery skin of the onion. Using a knife on a cutting board, cut the onion in half. Lay each onion half flat on the cutting board and chop.

5. Wash the celery stalks. Chop off and discard the ends. Thinly slice the celery.

6. Put the chopped onion and sliced celery in the bowl with the beans.

7. In a small bowl, whisk together the vinegar, olive oil, salt, and pepper to make a dressing.

8. Pour the oil-and-vinegar dressing over the beans.

9. Cover the bowl with plastic wrap.

10. Refrigerate the salad for 2 hours before serving.

····Sizzling Chicken Fajitas····

Time
30 to 35 minutes

Tools
shallow baking pan

knife

cutting board

3 small bowls

wire whip

aluminum foil

broiler pan

fork

oven mitts

Makes
4 fajitas

*Fajitas (fah-HEE-tahs) are tortillas wrapped around pieces of grilled meat or poultry and vegetables. They are usually served with **guacamole** (mashed avocado dip) and sour cream.*

Ingredients

½ pound (230 g) boneless chicken breast, thinly sliced

2 tablespoons (30 ml) lime juice

1 teaspoon (5 ml) salt

½ teaspoon (3 ml) black pepper

¼ head lettuce

1 ripe tomato

1 tablespoon (15 ml) chopped fresh cilantro

1 jalapeño pepper

2 tablespoons (30 ml) nonfat plain yogurt

2 tablespoons (30 ml) low-fat sour cream

⅛ teaspoon (1 ml) ground cumin

1 large onion

4 wheat tortillas

½ cup (120 ml) guacamole (optional)

Steps

1. Preheat the broiler.

2. Put the chicken breasts in a shallow baking pan, and sprinkle them with the lime juice, ½ teaspoon (3 ml) of the salt, and ¼ teaspoon (2 ml) of the pepper.

3. Let the chicken breasts marinate in the lime juice at room temperature until needed.

4. Wash the lettuce, tomato, cilantro, and jalapeño pepper.

5. Tear the lettuce into small pieces with your hands. Put in a small bowl and set aside.

6. Using a knife on a cutting board, slice the tomato. Put the slices in a small bowl and set aside.

7. Chop enough cilantro to make 1 tablespoon (15 ml).

• • • • •
*To **marinate** a food is to let it soak in a liquid called a **marinade**, which flavors and tenderizes the food.*
• • • • •

• • • • •
*Cilantro is the leaves of the herb **coriander**. It has a strong, distinctive flavor.*
• • • • •

8. Cut off the top and bottom of the jalapeño pepper. Remove and discard the ribs and seeds. Chop enough jalapeño pepper to make 1 teaspoon (5 ml).

9. Put the cilantro and jalapeño pepper in a small bowl, along with the yogurt, sour cream, cumin, ½ teaspoon (3 ml) salt, and ¼ teaspoon (2 ml) pepper. Whisk together, then set this mixture aside.

10. Remove the outer, papery skin of the onion. Using a knife on a cutting board, cut the onion in half. Lay each onion half flat on the cutting board and cut into ¼-inch (6-mm) slices.

11. Tightly wrap the tortillas in aluminum foil, then place them on the bottom rack of the oven to warm up.

12. Transfer the chicken from the lime juice marinade to a lightly oiled broiler pan, and top with the onions.

13. Pour the lime juice marinade down the drain.

14. Placing the broiler pan about 4 inches from the heat, broil the chicken for 3 to 4 minutes. *Keep an eye on the chicken at all times to make sure it does not over-cook!*

15. Using oven mitts, slide the oven rack out. Use a fork to turn the chicken breasts over, then broil for 3 to 4 minutes longer.

16. Remove the chicken and tortillas from the oven.

17. Cut the cooked chicken into thin strips.

18. To assemble the fajitas, fill each tortilla with chicken and onions, lettuce, and several tomato slices.

19. Roll up the tortillas and serve.

20. Top each tortilla with the sour cream mixture, and guacamole if desired.

• • • • •
When working with jalapeños or any other hot peppers, wear plastic gloves or cover your hands with sandwich bags so your skin does not sting from touching them. Be careful not to touch your skin, eyes, and face while working. Thoroughly clean knives and work surfaces when you finish.
• • • • •

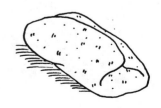

• Confetti Rice • • • • • • • • • • • • • • • • • •

Time
20 minutes to prepare
plus
30 minutes to cook

Tools
knife

cutting board

can opener

colander

small bowl

large saucepan

Makes
8 servings

Confetti Rice is simply rice with green and chili peppers, tomatoes, onions, and seasonings. It makes a very colorful dish.

Ingredients

1 medium onion

1 green pepper

1 28-ounce (794-g) can stewed tomatoes

1 4-ounce (113-g) can diced green chili peppers

¾ cup (180 ml) long-grain rice, uncooked

1 tablespoon (15 ml) Worcestershire sauce

1 teaspoon (5 ml) sugar

1 teaspoon (5 ml) chili powder

⅛ teaspoon (1 ml) pepper

several dashes bottled hot pepper sauce

1 cup (240 ml) water

1 tablespoon (15 ml) vegetable oil

Steps

1. Remove the outer, papery skin of the onion. Using a knife on a cutting board, cut the onion in half. Lay each onion half flat on the cutting board and chop.

2. Wash the green pepper. Cut the green pepper in half. Remove and discard the seeds and ribs from the inside of the green pepper. Cut the green pepper into strips, then chop.

3. Open the cans of stewed tomatoes and chili peppers. Using a colander, drain the liquid from the can of chili peppers only. Rinse the peppers, making sure all seeds have been removed.

4. Put the stewed tomatoes and drained chili peppers in a small bowl, along with the rice, Worcestershire sauce, sugar, chili powder, pepper, hot pepper sauce, and water. Set this mixture aside.

5. Put the oil in a large saucepan and heat on medium for 2 minutes.

6. Sauté the onions and green pepper in the oil for about 3 to 4 minutes.

7. Add the tomato and chili pepper mixture. Set the heat to high.

8. When the mixture boils, reduce the heat to low and simmer, covered, for 20 to 25 minutes or until the rice is tender and has absorbed all the liquid.

• • • • •
Sautéing vegetables such as these gives them more flavor.
• • • • •

Fast 'n' Easy Cornbread

Time
15 minutes to prepare
plus
35 to 40 minutes
to bake and cool

Tools
9-inch (22.5-cm) square
baking pan

large bowl

colander

medium bowl

Makes
9 pieces

*Cornbread can be eaten with meals
or as a snack. Put some jelly or jam on it
and try it for breakfast!*

Ingredients

vegetable oil cooking spray

1 cup (240 ml) cornmeal

1 cup (240 ml) all-purpose flour

¼ cup (60 ml) sugar

1 tablespoon (15 ml) baking powder

¼ teaspoon (2 ml) salt

1 cup (240 ml) canned low-sodium whole-kernel corn

2 eggs

1 cup (240 ml) skim or low-fat milk

¼ cup (60 ml) vegetable oil

Steps

1. Preheat oven to 425°F (220°C).

2. Spray the baking pan with vegetable oil cooking spray away from any heat.

3. Mix the cornmeal, flour, sugar, baking powder, and salt in a large bowl.

4. Open the can of corn, and empty it into a colander to drain off the liquid.

5. Mix the eggs, milk, oil, and corn in a medium bowl.

6. Pour the egg mixture into the cornmeal mixture, and mix the ingredients just until the batter is smooth.

7. Pour the batter into the baking pan.

8. Bake for 20 to 25 minutes or until golden brown.

9. Let cool for 15 minutes, then cut into 9 pieces.

*Don't overbeat the batter.
Overbeating causes the
cornbread to have holes
inside after baking.*

Rice Pudding

Rice is a popular grain in Mexican cooking. For this recipe, use leftover rice that has already been cooked.

Ingredients

1 egg

2 cups (480 ml) rice, cooked

2 cups (480 ml) skim or low-fat milk

⅓ cup (80 ml) sugar

1 teaspoon (5 ml) vanilla extract

¼ cup (60 ml) raisins

½ teaspoon (3 ml) cinnamon

Steps

1. Beat the egg with a fork in a small bowl.

2. Put the egg and all the remaining ingredients into the saucepan and stir with a wooden spoon.

3. Put the saucepan on a burner set to medium heat.

4. Bring the mixture to a boil, stirring frequently.

5. Reduce the heat to low and simmer for 5 minutes until thickened. Stir occasionally.

6. Remove the pan from the heat.

7. Carefully pour the pudding into a serving bowl or dessert bowls.

8. Let stand for 15 minutes, then chill for 2 hours before serving.

Time
15 minutes
plus
2¼ hours cooling time

Tools
fork

small bowl

saucepan

wooden spoon

serving bowl
or
8 dessert bowls

Makes
8 servings

PART 2

CENTRAL AND SOUTH AMERICA

CHAPTER 3
BRAZIL

Welcome to Brazil! South America's largest country, Brazil borders almost all the other South American countries.

BRAZIL

Brasilia ★

Brazilians eat a great deal of meat, especially beef, as cattle are raised in many areas of Brazil. Residents of Brazil's cities generally have a wide variety of foods available to them. But the situation is different for the many residents of rural areas. Beans, potatoes, rice, corn, and a starchy root called **cassava** (kah-SAH-vah) or **manioc** (mah-NEE-oahk) are the staples of their diet.

Breakfast in Brazil often includes fruit juice, fruit, and rolls filled with cheese or ham. Coffee with hot milk and sugar is the typical beverage for adults. Usually, the largest meal is lunch, starting with a soup or salad. The main course often includes rice, beans, vegetables, and a meat, chicken, or fish dish. Dessert may be a nut-cake or custard. The smaller evening meal typically includes salad, chicken or fish, and dessert.

Brazil's national dish, called **feijoada** (fay-HO-ah), is made of beef, black beans, sausage, and usually, rice. The national beverage, coffee, is also an important crop. Coffee comes from within the fruit harvested from coffee trees, which grow coffee

beans. The coffee beans are roasted and ground, then brewed to make fresh coffee. Use coffee in the following experiment to make a barometer.

HOW DOES A BAROMETER PREDICT THE WEATHER?

Materials
1 teaspoon (5 ml) instant coffee
1 cup (240 ml) water
straight-sided clear drinking glass
spoon
long-necked glass soda bottle
water-based marking pen

Purpose
To understand the relationship between air pressure and weather.

Procedure

1. Put the instant coffee and the water in the drinking glass. Stir until the water becomes colored.

2. Turn the bottle upside down and set it in the glass so that the mouth of the bottle rests just above the inside bottom of the glass and the bottle is straight up.

3. With the marking pen, mark the water level of the bottle on the outside of the glass.

4. Mark the water level daily for 1 week.

What Happened?
You have made a **barometer,** a device that measures air pressure. The air that surrounds you is made up of billions of **molecules** (very small particles of matter) that exert pressure as they speed around, causing what we call **atmospheric pressure** or **air pressure**. What's interesting about air pressure is that it is closely related to weather. When the water level in the bottle is

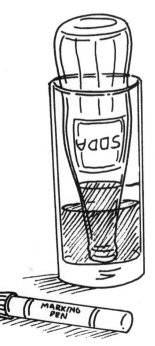

high, indicating high pressure, the air is pressing down hard on the water in the glass. This pushes the water farther up the bottle. High pressure predicts pleasant, dry weather. During times of low pressure, the air doesn't press as hard on the water in the glass, so the water level in the bottle is lower. A quick drop in air pressure usually indicates that rain, and possibly a storm, is coming.

The coffee used in the experiment colored the water, making it easier to see. Use more coffee to make an Iced Coffee and Chocolate Float and a batch of Mocha Cupcakes! Either of these will make a wonderful dessert for your Brazilian meal of Best Beef Kabobs and Fruited Rice.

Iced Coffee and Chocolate Float

Here's a fun recipe that combines a coffee flavor with vanilla ice cream and chocolate syrup to make a float.

Time
10 minutes

Tools
blender

4 tall glasses

Makes
4 servings

Ingredients

1 cup (240 ml) brewed or instant coffee, cooled

1 cup (240 ml) skim or 1% milk

2 tablespoons (30 ml) chocolate syrup

1 teaspoon (5 ml) vanilla extract

4 ice cubes

2 scoops vanilla ice cream

whipped cream (optional)

4 cinnamon sticks (optional)

Steps

1. Put the coffee, milk, chocolate syrup, and vanilla extract in the blender. Blend well.

2. Add the ice cubes and ice cream. Blend until mixture is smooth.

3. Pour into 4 tall glasses.

4. Garnish with whipped cream and cinnamon sticks, if desired.

Mocha-Flavored Cupcakes

Time
20 minutes to prepare
plus
1 hour 40 minutes
to bake and cool

Tools
muffin pan
(nonstick or regular)

paper cupcake cups
(optional)

large bowl

medium bowl

wooden spoon

oven mitts

wire rack

sandwich spreader

Makes
12 cupcakes

Mocha (MOH-kuh) is the flavor that results from blending coffee and chocolate or cocoa. This recipe blends instant coffee and chocolate chips to get a mocha flavor.

Ingredients

- 1 tablespoon (15 ml) shortening (if using regular muffin pan)
- 1¼ cups (300 ml) all-purpose flour
- 1 cup (240 ml) sugar
- 1½ teaspoons (8 ml) baking powder
- ½ teaspoon (3 ml) salt
- 1 egg
- ¾ cup (180 ml) skim or low-fat milk
- 1 tablespoon (15 ml) instant coffee
- ⅓ cup (80 ml) shortening, melted
- 1 teaspoon (5 ml) vanilla extract
- 1 cup (240 ml) semisweet chocolate chips
- ready-to-use frosting

Steps

1. Preheat oven to 400°F (200°C).
2. If using a regular muffin pan, grease the bottoms and sides of the muffin cups with shortening *or* line the pan with paper cupcake liners.
3. Mix the flour, sugar, baking powder, and salt in a large bowl.
4. Mix the egg, milk, coffee, melted shortening, and vanilla extract in a medium bowl.
5. Add the milk mixture all at once to the flour mixture in the large bowl.
6. Mix the ingredients with a wooden spoon until well blended.
7. Fold in the chocolate chips.

8. Using a large spoon, fill each muffin cup two-thirds full with batter.

9. Bake for 20 to 25 minutes or until golden brown.

10. Using oven mitts, remove the pan from the oven and set it on a wire rack to cool for 15 minutes.

11. Remove the cupcakes from the pan and let cool for 1 hour longer.

12. Ice the cupcakes, using a sandwich spreader and a ready-to-use frosting of your choice.

• • • • •
Don't ice any cake while it is warm, or the cake will stick to your spreader and the icing will become loose and runny.
• • • • •

Best Beef Kabobs

Time
1 hour to soak skewers
plus
25 to 30 minutes
to prepare
plus
10 to 15 minutes to cook

Tools
4 skewers
(bamboo or metal)

knife

cutting board

small bowl

wire whip

broiler pan

pastry brush

oven mitts

Makes
4 kabobs

• • • • •
*You can use skewers
made of bamboo, which
are disposable, or metal
ones, which can be
washed and reused.*
• • • • •

*Beef is plentiful in many areas of Brazil.
These kabobs use beef, vegetables, and a
flavorful sauce.* **Kabobs** *are small pieces of raw
meat, poultry, or seafood placed with vegetables
onto a skewer. Kabobs are usually broiled.
For greater flavor, brush the kabobs with the
sauce several times during cooking.*

Ingredients

2 small onions
2 green peppers
8 cherry tomatoes
1 pound (454 g) flank steak
1 cup (240 ml) pineapple
chunks, drained

¼ cup (60 ml) soy sauce
2 tablespoons (30 ml) honey
1 tablespoon (15 ml) olive oil
vegetable oil cooking spray

Steps

1. If using bamboo skewers, soak the skewers for 1 hour in warm water.

2. Remove the outer, papery skin of the onions. Using a knife on a cutting board, cut each onion in half. Lay each onion half flat on the cutting board and cut in half again.

3. Wash the green peppers and tomatoes.

4. Cut each green pepper in half. Remove and discard the seeds and ribs from the inside of the green peppers. Cut each green pepper half into 4 wedges.

5. Using a knife on a cutting board, cut the steak into 1½-inch (3.8-cm) cubes.

6. To assemble kabobs, put 1 steak cube, 1 onion piece, 2 pepper wedges, 1 tomato, and 1 pineapple chunk on a skewer. Repeat this pattern on the same skewer.

7. Fill the other 3 skewers as you did in step 6.

8. In a small bowl, whisk together the soy sauce, honey, and oil.

9. Preheat the broiler.

10. Away from any heat, spray the broiler pan with vegetable oil cooking spray.

11. Place the kabobs on the pan, and brush them with the soy sauce mixture.

12. Placing the kabobs about 6 inches (15 cm) from the heating element, broil the kabobs for 6 minutes. Keep an eye on the kabobs at all times to make sure they do not overcook!

13. Using oven mitts, slide the oven rack out. Turn the kabobs over and brush again with the soy sauce mixture.

14. Broil for about 5 more minutes.

15. Remove and serve.

Fruited Rice

Time
30 to 60 minutes (depending on type of rice)

Tools
medium saucepan with lid

knife

cutting board

small frying pan

serving dish

Makes
4 servings

Bananas, oranges, and grapefruit grow in Brazil. This recipe combines bananas and oranges with rice to make a favorite side dish.

Ingredients

1 cup (240 ml) brown or white rice

1 banana

1 orange

1 tablespoon (15 ml) margarine

¼ teaspoon (2 ml) cinnamon

dash nutmeg

Steps

1. Cook the rice according to the package directions.

2. While the rice is cooking, remove the skin from the banana, and peel the orange.

3. Using a knife on a cutting board, slice the banana into ¼-inch (6-mm) slices.

4. Cut the orange in half. Lay each orange half on the cutting board, and cut into ¼-inch (6-mm) slices.

5. Over medium heat, melt the margarine in a small frying pan.

6. Stir in the cinnamon and nutmeg. Turn off heat.

7. When the rice is done, add the banana and the seasoned margarine to the rice. Mix lightly.

8. Heat the mixture on low for 3 to 4 minutes.

9. Spoon the rice onto a serving dish. Garnish with the orange slices and serve.

PART 3

Europe

ITALY

Ciao! Welcome to Italy! As with many other countries, Italy's foods vary tremendously from region to region because of different climates, soils, and lifestyles. For example, cattle and dairy cows graze throughout northern Italy, so northern Italians eat much more beef and butter than people eat anywhere else in the country. Elsewhere, chicken, fish, veal, and pork are used more often than beef. In southern Italy, where wheat is harvested and olive trees grow, the people eat lots of pasta and olive oil.

When people think of Italian food, they often think of pizza and pasta. But pizza did not come from Italy. Pizza probably came from ancient Egypt, where they made flatbreads. The dough for making pasta—a paste made of flour, water, and salt—was probably developed in Italy before the thirteenth century.

There are more than a hundred different pasta shapes. Pastas are first boiled. Some are then served with a sauce, butter, or cheese to make them tastier. Others are layered into casseroles and baked with sauces. In northern Italy, where much corn and rice is grown, **polenta** (cornmeal mush) and rice share the spotlight with pasta.

Seafood is particularly popular along Italy's extensive coastline, where there are many different species of fish and shellfish. Sausage is also very popular, and there are many varieties in Italy, including pepperoni and salami. In the region of Bologna, the sausage is **mortadella** (mohr-tah-DELL-lah), a spicy sausage with cubes of animal fat and black peppercorns. Both mortadella and pepperoni are sliced thinly and eaten as appetizers. Appetizers are small bites of tasty foods eaten before the meal to stimulate the appetite.

Italian cuisine has a wide variety of vegetables and fruits including **finocchio** (rhymes with Pinocchio), a green vegetable called fennel in English. Other popular vegetables include artichokes, eggplant, peppers, and zucchini. Fresh figs, a popular fruit, are available in Italy year-round.

Olive oil is used for cooking in central and southern Italy, and it is the only oil used in salads. Olive oil is pale green and has a fruity, distinctive flavor.

Meals always include bread. Breads of different shapes and flavors are found in the various regions. For instance, in the Piedmont region, there are golden sticks of bread called **grissini** (gris-SEE-nee).

Cheeses of many types play a major part in Italian cooking. Mozzarella, a soft cheese, and ricotta, which looks like cottage cheese, both have a mild taste. Parmesan cheese, made in an area known as Parma, must be aged at least two years and has a sharper flavor. It is very hard and must be grated before being used.

Breakfast in Italy is similar to breakfast in other countries of Europe. Bread, rolls, and coffee with milk are served.

Lunch tends to be heartier than the evening meal. Appetizers such as marinated vegetables or slices of **prosciutto** (proh-SHOO-toh) (a spicy ham) with ripe figs begin lunch and supper.

Next come two courses. The first course includes pasta in broth or sauce, or soup, or risotto. **Risotto** (ree-SOT-to) is a creamy rice dish to which many different ingredients can be added. The second course is the meat, poultry, or fish course. Meat and poultry are usually broiled or roasted. At least two vegetable side dishes accompany this course. Vegetables are an important part of Italian cuisine and get much respect. Neither the first nor the second course is considered the main course; both are equally important.

After these courses, salad is served. In Italy, the typical salad dressing is olive oil, wine vinegar, and salt.

The last course is cheese with fruit. For special occasions, there are rich desserts such as ice cream, called **gelato** (jah-LAHT-to) in Italian.

Tomatoes are an important staple in Italian cooking. Tomatoes actually came to Italy from the New World—the Americas. In the following experiment, you will dry tomatoes to use on an Italian flatbread.

EXPERIMENT   WHY DO WE DRY FOODS?

Purpose

To understand how dehydration preserves foods.

• • • • •
A simple drying tray can be made by spreading cheesecloth over a wire rack.
• • • • •

Materials

1 pound (454 g) tomatoes
large saucepan
wooden spoon
large bowl
knife
cutting board
colander
drying tray
oven mitts
containers with tight-fitting lids

Procedure

1. Wash and dry the tomatoes.

2. Fill a large saucepan two-thirds full with water and put it on a burner. Set the heat to high.

3. When the water boils, use a wooden spoon to carefully place each tomato in the water.

4. After 3 to 4 minutes, turn off the heat and use the spoon to transfer the tomatoes to a large bowl.

5. Add enough cold water to the bowl to cover the tomatoes.

6. When the tomatoes are cool enough to handle, slip the skins off the tomatoes.

7. Using a knife on a cutting board, cut out the tomato cores.

8. Cut each tomato into thin slices.

9. Drain the tomatoes in a colander.

10. Preheat oven to 140°F (60°C).

11. Spread the tomatoes in one layer on the drying tray.

12. Put the drying tray in the oven, leaving the oven door open 1 to 2 inches (25 to 50 mm) to allow the air to circulate.

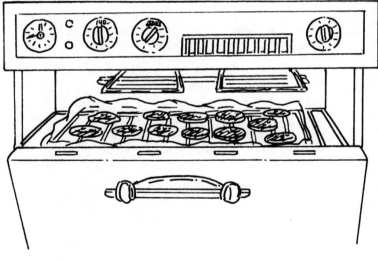

13. While the tomatoes dry (this will take 5 to 6 hours), turn the drying tray frequently. Watch closely during the last hour of drying, because tomatoes scorch easily.

14. When the tomatoes are leathery, hard, and crisp, use oven mitts to remove the tray from the oven. Let the tomatoes cool completely (about 1 hour).

15. Put the cooled dried tomatoes in small batches in containers with tight-fitting lids.

What Happened?

The lush, watery tomatoes became crisp and leathery due to the loss of water. For thousands of years people have used the heat of the sun to preserve foods by **dehydrating** (removing the water from) them. How does dehydration preserve food? Drying foods such as tomatoes removes the water that bacteria and molds need in order to grow. Thus, dried fruits and vegetables can stay edible for several months.

Use your dried tomato slices as a topping for the next recipe, Focaccia with Sun-Dried Tomatoes. Serve with an Antipasto Salad, followed by Cannoli for dessert, as a light Italian supper.

Focaccia with Sun-Dried Tomatoes

Focaccia (foh-KAH-chee-uh) is an Italian flatbread like the crust for a deep-dish pizza. Traditionally, this bread is topped with sun-dried tomatoes (use your dried tomato slices), onions, olives, herbs, and cheese, and served warm as a snack or side dish.

Time
40 minutes to prepare
plus
20 to 25 minutes
to bake

Tools
medium bowl

small bowl

knife

cutting board

small frying pan

colander

pizza pan

Makes
8 servings

Ingredients

1 package active dry yeast

1 cup (240 ml) lukewarm water

1 teaspoon (5 ml) sugar

1 teaspoon (5 ml) salt

4 tablespoons (60 ml) olive oil

2 to 3 cups (480 to 720 ml) all-purpose flour

12 dried tomato slices

1 tablespoon (15 ml) vegetable oil

1 small onion

½ cup (120 ml) black olives

1 cup (240 ml) shredded mozzarella cheese

1 teaspoon (5 ml) dried basil

Steps

1. Put the yeast and water in a medium bowl and stir.

2. Add the sugar, salt, and 2 tablespoons (30 ml) of the olive oil to the dissolved yeast and stir.

3. Add the flour to the yeast mixture in small amounts, mixing well with your hands after each addition. Stop adding flour when the dough no longer sticks in clumps to your hands or the bowl.

4. Transfer the dough to a lightly floured surface. Using your hands, knead the dough for 2 to 3 minutes.

5. Let the dough rest.

6. Put the dried tomatoes in a small bowl and cover with warm water. Set aside until needed.

7. Preheat the oven to 425°F (220°C).

• • • • •
Active dry yeast is dried granules of yeast that become active when put into water. Yeast is actually a fungus that lets off a gas that is responsible for making bread rise.
• • • • •

8. Remove the outer, papery skin of the onion. Using a knife on a cutting board, cut the onion in half. Lay each onion half flat on the cutting board and chop.

9. Slice the black olives.

10. Put the vegetable oil in a small frying pan and heat on medium for 2 minutes.

11. Sauté the onion and black olives in the oil for 3 minutes.

12. Drain the tomatoes in a colander

13. Press the dough evenly onto the pizza pan.

14. Drizzle the remaining olive oil over the dough.

15. Sprinkle evenly the tomatoes, cooked onion and olives, mozzarella cheese, and basil over the dough.

16. Bake for 20 to 25 minutes or until the bread is browned and the cheese is melted.

Antipasto Salad

In Italy, salad is often served as an appetizer, called **antipasto** (plural **antipasti**) in Italian. This antipasto uses the three colors of the Italian flag: red, white, and green.

Time
25 to 30 minutes

Tools
knife

cutting board

sandwich spreader

large platter

Makes
6 servings

Ingredients

5 stalks celery

1 green pepper

1 red pepper

2 tomatoes

½ cup (120 ml) softened low-fat cream cheese

2-oz. (56-g) jar pimiento pieces

½ pound (227 g) provolone cheese

1 head red leaf lettuce

12 green olives

salad dressing

Steps

1. Wash the celery, peppers, and tomatoes.
2. Using a knife on a cutting board, cut the peppers in half. Remove and discard the ribs and seeds. Cut the peppers into ¼-inch (6-mm) strips.
3. Cut the tomatoes into wedges.
4. Cut off and discard the leaves and ends of the celery stalks.
5. Spread the cream cheese into the celery stalks and dot with pimiento pieces. Cut each celery stalk in half lengthwise.
6. Using a knife on a cutting board, cut the provolone cheese into bite-sized cubes.
7. Wash the lettuce and dry well.
8. On a large platter, neatly arrange the lettuce leaves.
9. Arrange the celery stalks on the bed of lettuce so that they look like the spokes of a wheel.
10. Between the celery stalks, arrange the peppers, tomatoes, cheese cubes, and olives in a colorful pattern.
11. Serve with your favorite salad dressing.

Cannoli

Time
25 minutes to make filling
plus
1 hour chilling time
plus
20 minutes to fill

Tools
medium bowl

spoon

Makes
12 cannoli

• • • • •
*The filling needs to be
very cold so it is stiff
enough to be spooned
into the shells.*
• • • • •

The word cannoli *means "pipes." Cannoli are
little pipes of sweet pastry dough that have been
fried and stuffed with a creamy filling such as
ricotta cheese, pudding, or whipped cream. This
wonderful dessert comes from the island of Sicily
and is believed to date to prehistoric times.*

Ingredients

1 cup (240 ml) part-skim
ricotta cheese

½ cup (120 ml) confectioners'
sugar

1 cup (240 ml) mini chocolate
chips

12 cannoli shells

Steps

1. In a medium bowl, make the filling by mixing the
ricotta cheese, sugar, and chocolate chips.

2. Refrigerate the filling for 1 hour.

3. Spoon the chilled filling into the cannoli shells.

4. Refrigerate the
cannoli until
ready to serve.

CHAPTER 5

FRANCE

Bonjour! Welcome to France, the largest country in Europe. France has a population of over 56 million people living in 22 natural geographic regions derived from historic provinces.

Each province of France each has its own rich culture and heritage and has made notable contributions to French menus. For example,

- Brittany is given the credit for **crêpes** (kreps), the French version of pancakes. Crêpes can be stuffed with ingredients such as ham and cheese for a lunch or dinner main dish, or covered with fruit sauce or confectioners' sugar as a dessert or snack.

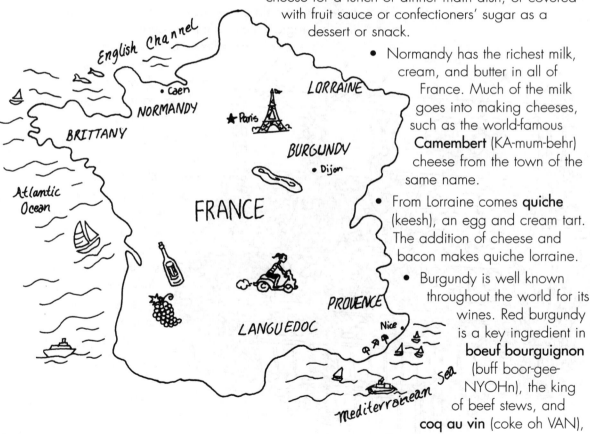

- Normandy has the richest milk, cream, and butter in all of France. Much of the milk goes into making cheeses, such as the world-famous **Camembert** (KA-mum-behr) cheese from the town of the same name.

- From Lorraine comes **quiche** (keesh), an egg and cream tart. The addition of cheese and bacon makes quiche lorraine.

- Burgundy is well known throughout the world for its wines. Red burgundy is a key ingredient in **boeuf bourguignon** (buff boor-gee-NYOHn), the king of beef stews, and **coq au vin** (coke oh VAN), a chicken casserole. From Dijon, the principal city of Burgundy, comes **Dijon** (dee-ZHOHn) **mustard,** a spicy mustard made by mixing ground mustard with wine vinegar. It is gaining popularity in the United States.

- The people of Languedoc love to make a dish called **cassoulet** (kass-soo-LAY), a rich stew made with goose or duck, pork or mutton, plus sausage and white beans.
- Down in the Mediterranean region of Provence, a popular dish is **bouillabaisse** (bwee-yah-BASE), a fish stew that also uses the favorite Mediterranean ingredients of olive oil, garlic, and tomatoes.

Spices and herbs differ with the climate and geography of each region, so the cooking in the high mountains of the Savoy tastes and smells of meadow plants, while similar dishes in other regions have another flavor, such as an apple flavor in Normandy, well-known for its apple orchards. In the south of France, garlic and tomatoes are used to flavor many dishes.

In the main towns of France, markets run by the towns still supply every local fruit, vegetable, cheese, and sausage, ready to eat. Local farmers come in to sell their fresh produce, posting their prices on small chalkboards.

The coastal areas of France are all rich sources of every type of seafood. Along the Atlantic, oysters abound and are shipped alive all over the country and across the English Channel to England. Other popular seafood includes clams, scallops, mussels, and sole.

The staff of life in France is bread. Crusty bread in varying shapes is bought daily. There are bakeries selling bread and other items wherever there is a community of people. Bread is the staple of breakfast. Served with butter and jam, and accompanied by a cup of coffee or hot chocolate, bread is a simple and quick-to-eat breakfast. The popular long, thin loaf of French bread is called a **baguette** (ba-GET). Instead of having part of a baguette for breakfast, the French may have **croissants** (kwah-SOHn), flaky, crescent-shaped rolls.

The main meal in France is likely to be served in the middle of the day, because many French employees break for lunch from noon to 2 P.M. Schoolchildren often return home for lunch as well.

Lunch starts with an appetizer, which is usually cold, such as freshly mixed vegetables or cold sliced potatoes. The main course usually consists of meat, poultry, or fish, such as pork chops with apples. Vegetables, such as glazed carrots, accompany the main dish.

After the main course, a salad of mixed fresh greens and a simple dressing of vinegar and oil is served to refresh the taste buds. Except on special occasions or Sunday, when dessert might be an apple tart, dessert consists of a plate of cheeses and a bowl of fresh fruit.

The evening meal is lighter than the main meal. It is less likely to include meat, fish, or fowl. Soup is a favorite at supper. An egg dish, such as an omelet or a quiche, may be the main course, along with a vegetable. Dessert is often fruit and cheese.

As you can tell, vegetables are an important part of the French diet. In the following experiment, you'll use celery to discover how plants get their nutrients.

EXPERIMENT HOW DO PLANTS TAKE IN NUTRIENTS?

Purpose
To observe osmosis in plants.

Materials
1 teaspoon (5 ml) red food coloring
tall drinking glass half filled with water
1 celery stalk with leaves

Procedure
1. Add the red food coloring to the glass of water.
2. Stand the celery stalk in the glass so that the leaves stick out the top of the glass.
3. Set the glass in a sunny window and let it sit through the rest of the day and through the night.
4. The next day, check the color of the leaves.

What Happened?
The leaves of the celery turn a reddish color like that of the water. Vegetables, such as celery, are plants, which absorb water and minerals from the soil. Minerals, such as iron and potassium, are nutrients that make the plant healthy food. After the water and minerals are absorbed into the plant, they flow into the plant's various cells. (A **cell** is the smallest unit of a living thing.) The process by which water flows across the plant's cell wall to enter the plant cell is called **osmosis.** In this experiment, you can actually see that the colored water traveled up into the celery and moved into its cells.

Use a fresh piece of celery in the Mixed Greens and Celery Salad. Serve your salad with a slice of Pick-a-Filling Quiche, then finish with Dessert Crêpes with Raspberry Sauce. *Bon appetit!*

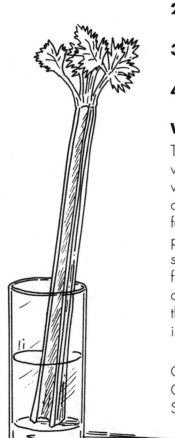

Mixed Greens and Celery Salad

This salad uses two types of lettuce that you may not have eaten before. See how they are is different from the more common iceberg lettuce. Then mix up some Dijon mustard with vinegar and oil to make a distinctly French dressing called vinaigrette (vin-eh-GRET).

Ingredients

½ head romaine lettuce

½ head red leaf lettuce

1 celery stalk

½ cup (120 ml) wine vinegar

2 teaspoons (10 ml) Dijon mustard

2 tablespoons (30 ml) olive oil

½ cup (120 ml) croutons

Steps

1. Wash both heads of lettuce and pat dry.

2. Using your hands, tear the lettuce into bite-sized pieces, discarding the not-so-tender spine of the romaine leaves.

3. Using a knife on a cutting board, cut off and discard the leaves and end of the celery stalk. Cut the celery into thin slices.

4. Put the lettuce and celery in a large bowl.

5. In a small bowl, make a vinaigrette by whisking together the vinegar, mustard, and oil.

6. Pour the vinaigrette over the vegetables. Toss well.

7. Sprinkle with croutons and serve.

Time
20 minutes

Tools
knife

cutting board

large bowl

small bowl

wire whip

Makes
6 servings

• • • • •
Vinaigrette *is a French word that means "vinegar dressing," a mixture of vinegar, oil, and seasonings.*
• • • • •

Time
25 minutes to prepare
plus
40 to 45 minutes to bake

Tools
medium bowl

knife

cutting board

medium saucepan

Makes
6 servings

*Quiche often includes vegetables or meat,
such as broccoli or bacon. In this recipe,
you can choose your own filling.*

Ingredients

3 eggs

1½ cups (360 ml) skim or
1% milk

¼ teaspoon (2 ml) ground
nutmeg

1 small onion

2 tablespoons (30 ml)
vegetable oil

½ cup (120 ml) chopped
frozen vegetable of your
choice, thawed

1 cup (4 ounces or 115 g)
grated Swiss and/or
Cheddar cheese

½ cup (120 ml) cooked
chicken, ham, or bacon

1 baked 9-inch (22.5 cm)
pie crust

Steps

1. Preheat oven to 325°F (165°C).

2. In a medium bowl, stir together the eggs, milk, and
nutmeg. Set this mixture aside.

3. Remove the outer, papery skin of the
onion. Using a knife on a cutting
board, cut the onion in half. Place
each onion half on the cutting
board and cut into ¼-inch (6-mm)
slices.

4. Place the oil in a saucepan
and heat on medium for 2
minutes.

5. Sauté the onion and thawed
vegetable until golden brown and
tender, about 5 minutes.

6. Let the sautéed vegetables cool slightly, then add to the egg mixture, along with the cheese and the chicken, ham, or bacon. Stir.

7. Pour the mixture into the pie crust.

8. Bake for 40 to 45 minutes or until a knife inserted near the center comes out clean. Watch the crust during baking. If it starts to get too brown, cover with aluminum foil.

Time
40 minutes

Tools
2 medium bowls

medium skillet

paper towels

colander

small bowl

medium saucepan

Makes
12 crêpes (6 servings)

What's great about this recipe, besides being delicious, is that you can make the crêpes and sauce ahead of time. Just reheat and serve. There is a special crêpe pan you can purchase for making crêpes, but it's not essential. A crêpe pan is simply a skillet with low sides and a wide cooking surface.

Ingredients

1 cup (240 ml) all-purpose flour

1½ cups (360 ml) milk

2 eggs

2 tablespoons (30 ml) plus ⅓ cup (80 ml) sugar

1 tablespoon (15 ml) plus 12 teaspoons (60 ml) vegetable oil

⅛ teaspoon (1 ml) salt

1 10-ounce (284-g) package frozen red raspberries, thawed

1 cup (240 ml) cranberry juice cocktail

4 teaspoons (20 ml) cornstarch

2 tablespoons (30 ml) margarine

2 teaspoons (10 ml) lemon juice

Steps

1. In a medium bowl, combine the flour, milk, eggs, 2 tablespoons (30 ml) of the sugar, 1 tablespoon (15 ml) of the oil, and the salt.

2. Put 1 teaspoon (5 ml) of the oil in a medium skillet and heat on medium for 2 minutes.

3. Spoon 3 tablespoons (45 ml) of batter into the skillet. Lift and tilt the skillet to spread the batter evenly.

4. Brown the crêpe on one side only, about 1 to 2 minutes, then turn the pan over above a paper towel so that the crêpe falls onto the towel.

5. Repeat steps 2 to 4 to make 11 more crêpes. Place a paper towel between each crêpe in the stack.

6. Drain the raspberries in a colander placed over a small bowl to save the liquid.

7. Add enough cranberry juice to the raspberry liquid to make 1½ cups (360 ml).

8. Mix the remaining ⅓ cup (80 ml) sugar and the cornstarch in a medium bowl. Add the raspberry liquid mixture. Stir.

9. Put the juice mixture in a medium saucepan and cook over medium heat till bubbly and thickened, stirring constantly.

10. Add the margarine, lemon juice, and raspberries to the saucepan and heat through. This is the raspberry sauce.

11. To serve, roll up 2 crêpes and place on a plate. Drizzle with raspberry sauce. Repeat for 5 more servings.

● ● ● ● ●
Cornstarch is a thickener that will keep the raspberry sauce from being too runny.
● ● ● ● ●

CHAPTER 6

GERMANY

Germany is in the center of Europe. Its borders have changed many times during its long history, but it has always covered a large and varied area, so it only makes sense that German eating habits vary with geographic location. Although there is a basic German cuisine, there have always been three culinary regions: the northern, central, and southern belts.

Northern German cooking is a reflection of its cold, damp climate. Hearty soups, roast duck and goose, and seafood from the North and Baltic Seas are popular foods. The food of northern Germany has been strongly influenced by that of Russia and Poland. Central German cooking is rich and filling. Some typical foods are pumpernickel bread and Westphalian ham. The southern style of cooking is lighter. In general, German foods are not heavily spiced.

Meats are an important part of the German diet. Germany is the land of the **wurst,** or sausage. The most famous sausage is the frankfurter, which is not called by that name in Germany! Germans enjoy roast pork and roast beef. One-dish meat meals, such as stews, are also popular.

In addition to meats, vegetables are a very important part of meals. The potato is the king of German vegetables. Potatoes are made into many different dishes, such as hot potato salad, potato pancakes, and potato dumplings.

A famous German dumpling dish, called **spaetzle** (SPET-zel), looks like noodles and is made from wheat flour.

Dried fruits are popular in German cooking. Dried apples, pears, and apricots may be part of a main dish. Dried fruits are often cooked in water to make stewed fruits.

Baking is a very important part of German heritage and cuisine. As in France, bread is the staff of life. It is plentiful and made in all shapes and sizes, and with all kinds of ingredients. White breads and dark breads, such as pumpernickel bread from Westphalia, are popular. Honey cakes, spice cakes, and fruit breads are the oldest forms of German baking yet still remain very popular. The most popular fruit bread, called **stollen** (SHTAH-luhn), is made at Christmastime and contains dried fruit and almonds.

Breakfast is often simply a selection of breads and rolls with butter and jam. Sometimes eggs, cheese, or cold cuts are also served. At school or at work, Germans often stop between nine and ten o'clock to have a sandwich, usually brought from home. We might call this a second breakfast!

Lunch is the main meal of the day. It is eaten at home when possible. During the weekend this meal is typically richer. Germans enjoy their "meat and potatoes" meals. Roasted meat, called **braten** (BRAH-tuhn) in German, is very popular. Soup, such as potato soup, may be served prior to the main course. Bread is always served. Fruit is generally served after the main course. Cakes and pastries are usually not served after meals but are eaten as part of the afternoon snack.

The afternoon snack, called **kaffee** (KAH-fee), is very important in German culture. It consists of cake or cookies with coffee, tea, or milk.

The name for the evening meal in German is **abend-brot** (AH-bunt-braht), which means "bread of the evening." This supper may consist of sandwiches or cold meat salads and vegetables. Desserts are not served.

Cabbage is an important vegetable in Germany. It is the main ingredient in **sauerkraut,** a traditional German food made from fermented cabbage. Red cabbage is popular in Germany as a side dish, but did you know that red cabbage juice can be used in scientific experiments? Go ahead and try this experiment!

EXPERIMENT

HOW CAN YOU TELL AN ACID FROM A BASE?

Purpose

To use cabbage juice to determine whether substances are acids or bases.

Materials

can opener
can of red cabbage
colander or strainer
small bowl
1-tablespoon (15-ml) measuring spoon
3 glass jars
1 tablespoon (15 ml) vinegar
1 tablespoon (15 ml) baking soda
1 tablespoon (15 ml) distilled water

Procedure

1. Open the can of red cabbage.

2. Using the colander, drain the cabbage juice into the bowl.

3. Put 2 tablespoons (30 ml) of the cabbage juice into each of 3 glass jars.

4. Add the vinegar to the first jar. What color did it turn?

5. Add the baking soda to the second jar. What color did it turn?

6. Add the distilled water to the third jar. What color did it turn?

What Happened?

Red cabbage juice is a **chemical indicator**, a substance that turns color in the presence of other substances, called acids or bases. When you added vinegar, which is an **acid** (a sour-tasting chemical), to the first jar, the cabbage juice turned redder. The redder the indicator gets, the stronger the acid. When you added baking soda, which is a **base** (a bitter-tasting chemical), the juice turned green. When you added distilled water, which is **neutral** (neither acid nor basic), it did not change the color of the juice.

Acids and bases are chemicals that have certain properties. Acids neutralize bases, while bases neutralize acids. Common acids in the kitchen include lemons, apple juice, black coffee, and of course, vinegar. Egg whites, like baking soda, are basic.

Even though red cabbage can be used as a chemical indicator, it's also good to eat! (But don't try to eat your experiment—it won't taste good.) Use fresh red cabbage in the Sweet-and-Sour Red Cabbage recipe and serve with Traditional German Sauerbraten, followed by Spice Cookies for dessert.

Sweet-and-Sour Red Cabbage

Time
50 minutes

Tools
knife

cutting board

medium saucepan with lid

colander

Makes
6 servings

Cooked red cabbage is a popular dish in northern Germany, where the climate is cold. Vinegar sweetened with sugar or honey is often used to make sweet-and-sour dressings and gravies for red cabbage and other vegetables.

Ingredients

½ medium head red cabbage

⅔ cup (160 ml) water

½ cup (120 ml) cider vinegar

6 strips bacon, cooked and chopped

2 tablespoons (30 ml) honey

Steps

1. Remove and discard the outer leaves of the cabbage.

2. Using a knife on a cutting board, cut the cabbage into thin slices.

3. In a medium saucepan, combine the cabbage, water, and vinegar.

4. Place the saucepan on a burner and set the heat to high.

5. When the water begins to boil, reduce the heat to low.

6. Cover the pan and simmer for 25 to 30 minutes or until the cabbage is tender.

7. Empty the cooked cabbage into a colander to drain the liquid, being careful not to splash any hot liquid on yourself.

8. Return the cabbage to the saucepan and stir in the bacon and honey.

9. Cook on low until heated, then serve.

Traditional German Sauerbraten

Sauerbraten *is a favorite German dish made from bottom round or other beef roast. Before the roast is cooked, it is marinated for several days in a mixture of vinegar and flavorings. The marinade tenderizes the meat and gives it flavor. Sauerbraten is usually served with red cabbage.*

Time
15 minutes to make marinade
plus
2 to 3 days to marinate
plus
3½ hours to prepare and cook
plus
15 minutes to make sauce

Tools
knife

cutting board

3 large bowls

plastic wrap

large frying pan

large Dutch oven

platter

colander

oven mitts

large saucepan

Makes
8 to 10 servings

Ingredients

1 onion

2 stalks celery

1 large carrot

3 pounds (1.3 kg) bottom round roast

2 teaspoons (10 ml) salt

½ teaspoon (3 ml) ground black pepper

2 cups (480 ml) cider vinegar

2 cups (480 ml) water

3 bay leaves

12 peppercorns

2 teaspoons (10 ml) ground cloves

½ teaspoon (3 ml) thyme

1 teaspoon (5 ml) mustard seed

¼ cup (60 ml) sugar

½ cup (120 ml) all-purpose flour

2 tablespoons (30 ml) oil

¼ cup (60 ml) seedless raisins

12 gingersnaps, crushed

Steps

1. Remove the outer, papery skin of the onion. Using a knife on a cutting board, cut the onion in half. Lay each onion half flat on the cutting board and chop.

2. Wash the celery and carrot.

3. Cut off and discard the leaves and ends of the celery stalks. Cut the celery into thin slices.

4. Slice the carrot.

5. Place the roast in a large bowl. Then add the vegetables, salt, ground pepper, vinegar, water, bay leaves, peppercorns, cloves, thyme, mustard seed, and sugar.

6. Cover the bowl with plastic wrap and marinate the meat in the refrigerator for 2 to 3 days. Turn the roast several times each day with a large fork.

7. Transfer the meat to a clean bowl. Save the marinade.

8. Sprinkle the meat with the flour.

9. Put the oil in a large frying pan and heat on medium for 2 minutes.

10. Brown the meat in the oil on all sides.

11. Put the meat and the marinade in a large Dutch oven.

12. Put the Dutch oven on the burner and set the heat to low. Simmer for 3 hours or until tender.

13. Using oven mitts, remove the Dutch oven from the heat. Transfer the meat to a platter.

14. Strain the liquid by pouring it through a colander into a large bowl.

15. Make a sauce by putting the strained liquid, raisins, and gingersnaps in a large saucepan and stirring until thick.

16. Slice the meat and serve with the sauce.

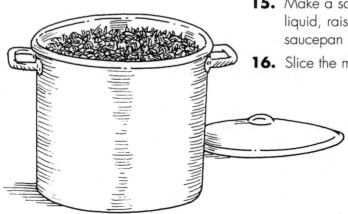

Spice Cookies

Spice Cookies are a favorite German cookie. These cookies are made by making a roll of dough ahead of time and refrigerating it. The roll is later sliced into cookies and baked.

Ingredients

- ½ cup (120 ml) margarine
- ½ cup (120 ml) vegetable shortening
- 2¼ cups (540 ml) all-purpose flour
- ½ cup (120 ml) white sugar
- ½ cup (120 ml) brown sugar
- 1 egg
- 1 teaspoon (5 ml) ground cinnamon
- ½ teaspoon (3 ml) baking soda
- ½ teaspoon (3 ml) vanilla extract
- ¼ teaspoon (1 ml) ground nutmeg
- ¼ teaspoon (1 ml) ground cloves
- ½ cup (120 ml) chopped nuts

Steps

1. In a medium bowl, beat the margarine and shortening with an electric mixer on medium speed for half a minute.

2. Turn the mixer off and add the following to the bowl: 1 cup (240 ml) of the flour, white sugar, brown sugar, egg, cinnamon, baking soda, vanilla, nutmeg, and cloves.

3. Turn the mixer to medium speed and beat the ingredients until they are completely combined.

4. Beat in the rest of the flour a little at a time until it is completely mixed in.

5. Using a wooden spoon, stir the nuts into the dough.

Time
25 minutes to make dough
plus
1 day chilling time
plus
30 to 40 minutes to bake

Tools
medium bowl

electric mixer

wooden spoon

plastic wrap

knife

cutting board

cookie sheet

oven mitts

spatula

wire rack

Makes
5 dozen

• • • • •

Spice cookies get their name from the variety of spices that flavor them.

• • • • •

6. Transfer the dough to a lightly floured surface. Using your hands, shape the dough into two 7-inch-long (18-cm) round rolls.

7. Wrap each roll in plastic wrap. Refrigerate for 1 day.

8. When ready to bake, preheat the oven to 375°F (190°C).

9. Using a knife on a cutting board, cut each roll of cookie dough into ¼-inch (6-mm) slices.

10. Place slices 1 inch (25 mm) apart on an ungreased cookie sheet.

11. Bake in batches for about 8 minutes per batch or until the edges are golden.

12. Using oven mitts, remove cookie sheet from oven. Let cookies cool on cookie sheet for 1 minute. Then remove with a spatula and transfer to a wire rack to cool.

CHAPTER 7

SPAIN

Spain is attached to France, and to Europe, by a band of mountains in the northeast called the Pyrenees. At its southern tip, Spain is separated from Africa by the Strait of Gibraltar. To the west is the country of Portugal. The mountains in Spain have served to separate different regions and cultures. As in many countries, each region has its own cuisine. For example, in the Basque Provinces, along the Bay of Biscay, seafood is served often. In fact, throughout Spain, seafood is king. Chicken is also a frequent ingredient in Spanish cooking. Beef is served most often in northern Spain, where there are pastures for cattle.

Fruits and vegetables are important foods. The city of Valencia is well known for its Valencia oranges. The region of Catalonia, along Spain's northeastern coast, provides much of Spain with fresh fruits, such as pears, peaches, melons, grapes, and cherries. Olives are an important crop in southern Spain. Olives are used to make olive oil, which is used in salads and in cooking.

Some important regional dishes include these.

- In Madrid, a well-liked food is **cocido** (koh-SEE-doh), a rich dish of boiled beef.

- Rice is very popular along the east coast of Spain and is used to make **paella** (pah-AY-yah), a rice stew made with chicken, shellfish, and vegetables.

- A regional specialty in southern Spain, where it is hot and dry, is **gazpacho** (gahs-PAH-cho), a cold soup made of tomatoes, green peppers, cucumber, and garlic.

- Estremadura in western Spain is known for its spicy red sausage, called **chorizo** (choh-REE-soh), and for thin, wild asparagus.

- In the region of Catalonia, garlic is used to flavor many dishes. The residents also enjoy eating **calamares,** or squid, from the Mediterranean Sea.

- In the region of Galicia, Spain's most important fishing area, the residents make **empanada** (em-pah-NAH-dah), a thick seafood or meat pie that is often served cold.

Open-air markets supply every local fruit, vegetable, cheese, chicken, and seafood. Most Spanish cheeses are white, smooth, and mild in flavor. Bread is purchased daily at bakeries.

For breakfast, most Spaniards eat a small meal of bread or rolls with butter and jelly. Adults drink **cafe con leche,** coffee with milk and lots of sugar.

The big meal of the day is usually eaten in the afternoon between two and four o'clock. During this time, called **siesta**, schools and businesses close down so that families can have dinner together.

Dinner often starts with soup, such as lentil soup, and then a salad, which may include cheese, hard-cooked egg, and olives. Salad is followed by the main course, which may be paella or chicken with rice. Vegetables accompany the main dish or may be served as a separate course. Dessert is often cheese and fruit. Sweets are saved for an evening snack.

The evening meal, supper, is served quite late. It is a lighter meal, consisting often of soup with an omelet or sandwich. Salad may be served as well, along with fruit and cheese to finish.

Flan (flahn), a popular Spanish dessert, is actually caramel custard. Try the following experiment to learn more about custards.

WHAT HAPPENS WHEN YOU COOK CUSTARD?

Materials

Baked Custard

Ingredients

  3 eggs

  1½ cups (360 ml) milk

  ⅓ cup (80 ml) sugar

  1 teaspoon (5 ml) vanilla

Tools

  see page 75

Stirred Custard

Ingredients

  3 eggs

  2 cups (480 ml) milk

  ¼ cup (60 ml) sugar

  1 teaspoon (5 ml) vanilla

Tools

  medium saucepan

  metal spoon

  large bowl of ice water

  medium bowl

  plastic wrap

Purpose

To understand the difference between a sol and a gel.

Procedure

1. Prepare 4 individual baked custards using the ingredients under "Baked Custard" on page 73, and by following steps 3 to 13 of the recipe for Flan in this chapter.

2. Prepare the stirred custard.

- Combine the eggs, milk, and sugar in a medium saucepan. Cook over medium heat, stirring constantly until the egg mixture just coats a metal spoon.

- Remove the pan from the heat. Stir in the vanilla.

- Cool the custard quickly by setting the saucepan in a large bowl of ice water for 3 minutes, stirring constantly.

- Pour the custard into a medium bowl, cover with plastic wrap, and refrigerate.

3. On a small plate, put one big spoonful each of baked custard and stirred custard. Do they look different? Taste them. Do they taste different?

What Happened?

Custard is a mixture of milk and eggs. Although custards are made with the same ingredients, either a sol or a gel may form when the mixture is heated, depending on what happens during the cooking process. Continuous stirring during cooking results in a stirred custard, called a **sol.** Stirred custards are creamy. When the mixture is baked in the oven without any agitation, the custard **gels** (becomes solid) and is called a baked custard. In both cases, the protein in the eggs thickens the custard.

Serve Flan for dessert after a Spanish meal of One-Pot Paella and Pimiento Drop Biscuits.

Flan is the Spanish name for caramel custard. What makes this custard different is the caramel sugar that covers it.

Ingredients

½ cup (120 ml) plus ⅓ cup (80 ml) sugar

¼ cup (60 ml) water

2 cups (480 ml) milk

¼ teaspoon (2 ml) vanilla extract

¼ teaspoon (2 ml) rum extract

2 eggs

2 egg yolks

1 cup (240 ml) whipped cream

Steps

1. Heat ½ cup (120 ml) of the sugar and the water in a 3-quart (3-L) saucepan over medium heat until the mixture is light brown. This is caramel sugar.

2. Coat the bottom of each custard cup with about 1 teaspoon (5 ml) of caramel sugar by swishing it around.

3. In a medium saucepan, heat the milk over medium heat until steam comes off the top and the milk is about to simmer.

4. Stir in the remaining ⅓ cup sugar and continue to stir until the sugar dissolves.

5. Let the milk cool for 10 minutes.

6. Stir the vanilla and rum extracts into the cooled milk.

7. Preheat the oven to 350°F (175°C).

8. In a medium bowl, beat the eggs and egg yolks with an electric mixer on high speed until bubbly, about 3 minutes.

9. Pour the eggs into the cooled milk mixture and stir.

Time
60 minutes

Tools
3-quart (3-L) saucepan

8 custard cups

medium saucepan

medium bowl

electric mixer

ladle

9-by-13-inch (22.5-by-32.5-cm) baking pan

oven mitts

table knife

Makes
8 servings

•••••
*Water is poured around
the custard cups to
protect the custard
from the high oven
temperature. Overheated
custard curdles and
becomes watery.*
•••••

10. Ladle the mixture into the caramel-coated custard cups.

11. Place the custard cups in a baking pan. Pour ½ inch (13 mm) of water into the pan.

12. Bake for 20 to 25 minutes or until a knife inserted into the custard comes out clean.

13. Using oven mitts, remove the custard cups from the pan and let cool for 30 minutes.

14. Unmold the custards by running a table knife around the edges and turning them over onto a plate.

15. Keep refrigerated until ready to serve. Decorate with whipped cream.

One-Pot Paella

Paella is Spain's national dish.
It is a rice dish cooked with a variety of
meats, sausage, poultry, shellfish, or game.
It also includes various vegetables, such as
peas and tomatoes, and is flavored with garlic,
onions, and saffron. The exact ingredients of
this dish vary from place to place.

Time
50 to 60 minutes

Tools
knife

cutting board

large saucepan

Makes
6 servings

Ingredients

1 medium onion

1 green pepper

1 red pepper

1 yellow pepper

2 boneless chicken breasts

¼ cup (60 ml) olive oil

1 teaspoon (5 ml) saffron

2 cups (480 ml) chicken broth

10½-ounce (300-g) can baby shrimp, drained

12 scallops

1 cup (240 ml) frozen peas

½ cup (120 ml) frozen corn

1 cup (240 ml) chopped plum tomatoes

salt and pepper to taste

3 cups (700 ml) rice, cooked

• • • • •
*Saffron turns foods
yellow and has an
exotic flavor.*
• • • • •

Steps

1. Remove the outer, papery skin of the onion. Using a knife on a cutting board, cut the onion in half. Lay each onion half flat on the cutting board and chop.

2. Wash the green, red, and yellow peppers. Cut each pepper in half. Remove and discard the seeds and ribs. Cut each pepper into strips, then chop.

3. Measure ½ cup (120 ml) of each color pepper.

4. Cut the chicken breasts into ½-inch (13-mm) slices. Cut the slices again in the opposite direction to make cubes.

5. Put the oil in a large saucepan and heat on medium for 2 minutes.

6. Sauté the onion and peppers in the oil until tender.

7. Add the saffron and cubed chicken to the saucepan. Sauté until the chicken is completely cooked.

8. Add the chicken broth, shrimp, and scallops. Set the heat to high. Once the mixture boils, reduce the heat to low and simmer, uncovered, for 10 minutes.

9. Add the peas, corn, tomatoes, and salt and pepper. Simmer for 15 more minutes.

10. Add the rice and stir until heated through. Serve immediately.

Pimiento Drop Biscuits

*Pimientos originated in Spain.
They are small, sweet red chilis that
add color to salads and vegetable dishes.
In this recipe, they add color to biscuits.*

Ingredients

2 cups (480 ml) all-purpose flour

1 tablespoon (15 ml) baking powder

½ teaspoon (3 ml) baking soda

¼ teaspoon (1 ml) salt

¼ cup (60 ml) margarine, chilled

¾ cup (180 ml) low-fat buttermilk

3 tablespoons (45 ml) chopped pimientos, drained

Steps

1. Preheat the oven to 400°F (200°C).

2. Put the flour, baking powder, baking soda, and salt in a medium bowl. Mix well.

3. Using a table knife on a cutting board, cut the margarine into small pieces. Put the margarine in the bowl with the flour mixture.

4. Cut in the margarine with a pastry blender, *or,* holding a table knife in each hand, draw the knives across each other to cut through the margarine and dry ingredients. Keep cutting until the mixture is in pieces about the size of small peas.

5. Add the buttermilk and stir just until the dry ingredients are moistened.

6. Fold in the pimientos.

7. Knead the dough on a lightly floured surface.

Time
20 minutes to make dough
plus
15 minutes to bake
and cool

Tools
medium bowl

2 table knives

cutting board

pastry blender

3-inch (7.5-cm) round biscuit cutter
or
juice glass

cookie sheet

oven mitts

Makes
12 biscuits

• • • • •
*Knead for only about
30 seconds. Biscuit dough
should be soft and a
little stretchy, but not
sticky. Overkneading
toughens the biscuits, so
don't overdo it.*
• • • • •

8. Pat the dough out to a ½-inch (13-mm) thickness. Cut the biscuits out with a 3-inch (7.5-cm) round cutter (or use a juice glass).

9. Place the biscuits 1 inch (25 mm) apart on an ungreased cookie sheet.

10. Bake for 10 to 12 minutes or until golden brown.

11. Using oven mitts, remove from the oven and let cool for a few minutes before serving.

PART 4

THE MIDDLE EAST

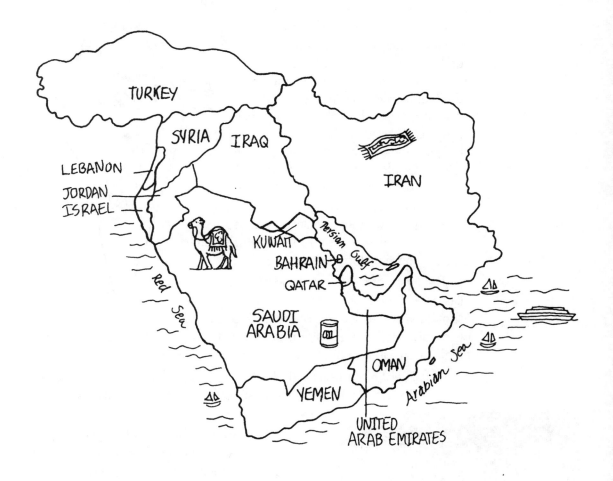

CHAPTER 8

ISRAEL

The state of Israel, located at the eastern edge of the Mediterranean Sea, was established in 1949 as a homeland for the Jewish people. Israel's residents have come from all around the world, and each nationality has brought its favorite dishes. Jews from Austria brought **Wiener schnitzel**, sliced veal that is breaded and fried, which has become a popular Israeli dish. After World War II Hungarian Jews brought many goulash recipes. **Goulash** is a highly seasoned stew of beef, veal, or pork made with onions, potatoes, tomatoes, peppers, and dumplings. Jews from the United States brought typical American foods, such as hamburgers and hot dogs.

The types of foods that Israelis eat are also influenced by Jewish tradition and dietary laws. Many Jewish people do not eat pork or shellfish. Many also do not eat dairy products at the same meal with meat. Each meal is considered either a dairy meal or a meat meal.

Israelis eat more poultry and fish than beef, which must be imported and is therefore expensive. The most popular fish is carp, a freshwater fish.

Israel grows many fruits and vegetables. Israelis eat a wide variety of vegetables, including eggplant, squash, turnips, cabbage, peppers, celery, cauliflower, onions, and garlic. Salads are a staple, and the most popular salad dressing is lemon and oil.

Tea and coffee both are popular in Israel. Carbonated drinks, made with bubbly water and sweet syrups, are a cool refreshment during the hot summer months.

Special foods are often eaten during religious holidays. For example, during Hanukkah, oil-fried foods such as potato pancakes, called **latkes** (LAHT-kehs), are eaten.

Breakfast is typically a hearty meal and may include eggs, fruit such as grapefruit, bread with margarine and jelly, and coffee. A midmorning snack may include doughnuts or **felafel** (feh-LAH-fel), an ancient dish of the Arabian peninsula that is made of pita bread filled with fried balls of a chickpea and cracked wheat mixture. Felafel and latkes are popular snacks sold on the streets of Israeli cities.

A large meal is often eaten in early or mid-afternoon. This often includes soup or salad as an appetizer, then a main course of meat, poultry, or fish with vegetables. Salads are made with whatever fresh vegetables are available. The main course might be Wiener schnitzel or fish with a vegetable, such as baked corn and carrots. When the large meal is eaten at midday, the evening meal is light and may be meatless.

Israelis call dessert "the final dish." Fresh fruit and date bars or spiced orange wedges are most common. Sweet desserts, such as cookies or cakes, are usually reserved for special days.

Potatoes, grown in central Israel, are an important Israeli food that is used to make potato pancakes and other dishes. Try the following experiment to learn about the specific gravity of potatoes.

HOW CAN YOU DETERMINE THE SPECIFIC GRAVITY OF POTATOES?

Purpose

To understand the concept of specific gravity.

Materials

knife
cutting board
1 small baking potato
1 red-skinned new potato
4 tablespoons (60 ml) salt
2¾ cups (660 ml) water
2 small bowls

Procedure

1. Using a knife on a cutting board, cut each potato in half.

2. Place 2 tablespoons (30 ml) of salt and 1⅜ cup (330 ml) of water in each bowl.

3. Put half the baking potato in one bowl and half the new potato in the other bowl.

4. Which potato sinks to the bottom of the bowl?

What Happened?

The baking potato sinks to the bottom of the bowl, while the new potato floats on the water. The baking potato has a higher specific gravity than the new potato. **Specific gravity** is a comparison of the density of an object to the density of water. The **density** of any object is the mass, or amount of material, that it contains compared to its volume. Baking potatoes contain a lot of starch but not very much water, whereas new potatoes contain little starch but a lot of water. Thus, new potatoes are less dense than baking potatoes. This is why the new potato floated on the salty water and the baking potato sank.

Save your baking potato to make Potato Pancakes. Then try the Cheese Blintzes, and the delicious Lemony Coconut Cookies.

Potato Pancakes, or latkes, are a great way to enjoy potatoes! These latkes use an ingredient called matzo meal. **Matzo meal** is finely ground matzo, an unleavened bread that looks like a cracker. Matzo is eaten during the Jewish holiday of Passover and also all year round. Matzo meal is frequently used in Israeli dishes in place of flour or bread crumbs.

Time
50 to 60 minutes

Tools
vegetable brush

knife

peeler

cutting board

medium saucepan

colander

large bowl

potato masher
or
electric mixer

7- or 8-inch
(17.5- or 20-cm)
nonstick frying pan

paper towels

Makes
6 pancakes

Ingredients

2 baking potatoes

4 eggs

1 cup (240 ml) matzo meal

½ teaspoon (3 ml) salt

1 cup (240 ml) water

1 tablespoon (15 ml) margarine

sour cream and applesauce
or fruit or jam

Steps

1. Scrub the potatoes with a brush under running water. Remove the eyes and any decayed areas with a knife. Peel the potatoes with a peeler. Using a knife on a cutting board, cut the potatoes into quarters.

2. Put the potatoes in the saucepan and add enough water to cover.

3. Bring the water to a boil over medium-high heat. Boil the potatoes until tender, about 20 to 30 minutes.

4. Using a colander, drain off the water and put the potatoes in a large bowl.

5. Mash the potatoes with a potato masher or electric mixer.

6. Mix the eggs, matzo meal, salt, and water with the mashed potatoes.

7. With your hands, shape the mashed potato mixture into 6 oval pancakes. Each pancake should be about 4 inches long and 3 inches wide.

8. Melt the margarine in a 7- or 8-inch (17.5- or 20-cm) nonstick frying pan over medium heat.

9. Panfry the pancakes until they are brown on each side.

10. Drain the pancakes on paper towels.

11. Top with sour cream and applesauce, or try your favorite fruit or jam.

•••••••••••••• •••• Cheese Blintzes •••• ••••••••••••••

Blintzes are made by making thin pancakes, then filling them with a cheese mixture and browning in a frying pan. Blintzes are traditionally served with sour cream and fruit.

Ingredients

3 eggs

¾ cup (180 ml) skim milk

½ teaspoon (3 ml) salt

½ cup (120 ml) flour

4 ounces (113 g) light cream cheese, softened

8 ounces (227 g) 2% low-fat cottage cheese

¼ cup (60 ml) raisins

12 teaspoons (60 ml) plus 1 tablespoon (15 ml) margarine

½ cup (120 ml) reduced-fat sour cream

1 large jar applesauce

Steps

1. Combine 2 of the eggs and the milk, salt, and flour in a medium bowl. Stir until most of the lumps have disappeared. Let stand for 15 minutes while you make the cheese filling.

2. In a medium bowl, combine the cream cheese, cottage cheese, and the remaining egg. Stir until smooth, then stir in the raisins.

3. Melt 1 teaspoon (5 ml) of the margarine in a 7- or 8-inch (17.5- or 20-cm) nonstick frying pan.

4. Pour ¼ cup (60 ml) of batter into the pan and tilt it quickly to coat the bottom. The pancake will be very thin. Cook the pancake on one side only, until the surface is bubbly and the bottom is lightly browned, about 2 to 3 minutes.

Time
60 minutes

Tools
2 medium bowls

7- or 8-inch
(17.5- or 20-cm)
nonstick frying pan

spatula

waxed paper

Makes
12 blintzes

• • • • •
Do not overstir the batter, or the pancakes will be tough.
• • • • •

ISRAEL ••• **87**

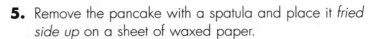

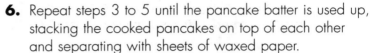

5. Remove the pancake with a spatula and place it *fried side up* on a sheet of waxed paper.

6. Repeat steps 3 to 5 until the pancake batter is used up, stacking the cooked pancakes on top of each other and separating with sheets of waxed paper.

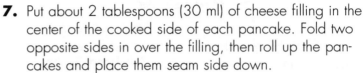

7. Put about 2 tablespoons (30 ml) of cheese filling in the center of the cooked side of each pancake. Fold two opposite sides in over the filling, then roll up the pancakes and place them seam side down.

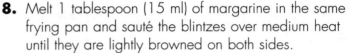

8. Melt 1 tablespoon (15 ml) of margarine in the same frying pan and sauté the blintzes over medium heat until they are lightly browned on both sides.

9. Serve with sour cream and applesauce.

Lemony Coconut Cookies

Like Potato Pancakes, this recipe also uses matzo meal in place of flour. If you like lemon and coconut, this is the cookie for you!

Ingredients

5 eggs
1½ cups (360 ml) sugar
1 cup (240 ml) matzo meal
2 cups (480 ml) shredded coconut
2 lemons
¼ teaspoon (2 ml) salt

Steps

1. Preheat the oven to 400°F (200°C).

2. Using a wire whip, beat the eggs in a medium bowl.

3. Add the sugar and continue beating until the mixture is smooth and creamy.

4. Fold in the matzo meal and coconut with a rubber spatula.

5. Using a knife on a cutting board, cut the 2 lemons in half. Squeeze their juice into the batter. Don't throw out the lemons.

6. Using the tiny holes on a grater, grate the yellow part of the rind of both lemons.

7. Fold the grated lemon peel into the batter, along with the salt.

8. Drop the mixture by teaspoonfuls onto a greased cookie sheet. Allow room for the batter to spread.

9. Bake in batches for 15 minutes per batch or until golden.

10. Using oven mitts, remove cookie sheet from oven. Let cookies cool for 3 minutes before removing with a metal spatula and placing on wire racks to cool.

Time
15 minutes to prepare
plus
30 minutes to bake

Tools
wire whip
medium bowl
rubber spatula
knife
cutting board
grater
cookie sheet
teaspoon
oven mitts
metal spatula
wire rack

Makes
24 cookies

• • • • •
The yellow rind of lemons is used in baking to give a lemony flavor. Don't grate the white part of the rind, as it has a bitter flavor.
• • • • •

PART 5

Asia

Arctic Ocean

RUSSIA

KAZAKHSTAN

MONGOLIA

NORTH KOREA

JAPAN

SOUTH KOREA

Pacific Ocean

TURKEY

AFGHANISTAN

CHINA

MIDDLE EAST

IRAQ

IRAN

BHUTAN

TAIWAN

PAKISTAN

NEPAL

PHILIPPINES

SAUDI ARABIA

OMAN

INDIA

MYANMAR (BURMA)

LAOS

VIETNAM

YEMEN

BANGLADESH

THAILAND

BRUNEI

Arabian Sea

CAMBODIA

MALAYSIA

N
W   E
S

SRI LANKA

INDONESIA

Indian Ocean

SINGAPORE

CHAPTER 9

NDIA

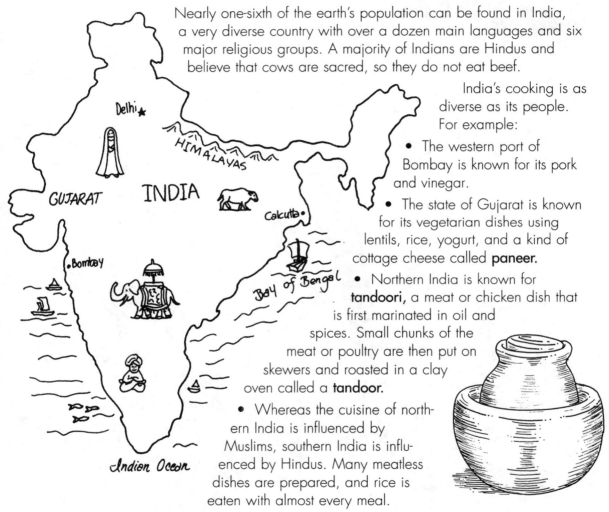

Nearly one-sixth of the earth's population can be found in India, a very diverse country with over a dozen main languages and six major religious groups. A majority of Indians are Hindus and believe that cows are sacred, so they do not eat beef.

India's cooking is as diverse as its people. For example:

- The western port of Bombay is known for its pork and vinegar.

- The state of Gujarat is known for its vegetarian dishes using lentils, rice, yogurt, and a kind of cottage cheese called **paneer.**

- Northern India is known for **tandoori,** a meat or chicken dish that is first marinated in oil and spices. Small chunks of the meat or poultry are then put on skewers and roasted in a clay oven called a **tandoor.**

- Whereas the cuisine of northern India is influenced by Muslims, southern India is influenced by Hindus. Many meatless dishes are prepared, and rice is eaten with almost every meal.

The staples of the Indian diet are rice, beans, lentils, and bread. Rice is usually served steamed and mixed with flavorings. Basmati rice has a nutty flavor and is used for special occasions. Dried beans, lentils, and split peas are popular in vegetarian dishes. Indian breads include **chapatis** (chah-PAH-tees), a round flatbread made of whole wheat flour, and **naan,** a bread that uses yeast to make it rise a little.

Most of the meat dishes in India use chicken or lamb, which are prepared in a number of ways. They may be used to make a spicy stew, marinated and grilled, cooked in yogurt or cream, sautéed and baked, or shaped into meatballs.

Vegetables are often fried in vegetable oil with spices and served without any sauce. Vegetables may also be mashed and shaped into balls and fried. Onions, garlic, and ginger are used for flavoring. Popular vegetables include cauliflower, okra, potatoes, and spinach. **Okra** is a long, green vegetable with edible seeds. It is served by itself or used in stews and soups.

Most Indian main dishes are accompanied by chutneys or raitas. **Chutney** is a relish made from fruits, vegetables, and herbs. **Raita** (RYE-tah) is grated vegetables mixed with yogurt. Chutney may be cooked, but raita is not.

Indian cooking uses many strong spices. The heart of Indian cooking is the combination of spices that gives each dish its unique flavor. Spices frequently used to create a special taste include the following:

- Cinnamon, made from the bark of the cinnamon tree.

- Cloves, the dried flower buds of the clove tree.

- Fenugreek, an ancient herb with yellow seeds that taste like celery.

- Ginger, a bumpy root with light brown skin and a hot, spicy flavor.

- Mace, made from the seed covering of the nutmeg tree.

- Saffron, made from a certain type of crocus flower. It is very expensive to make. Saffron turns food a vivid yellow color.

- Turmeric, made from the roots of an herb. Like saffron, it turns foods a vivid yellow, but it does not taste like saffron.

In addition to spices, garlic, onions, and chilis are popular. Chilis are green or red peppers that are very hot.

Tea, a very popular drink in India, is grown on plantations. Indian tea is made by boiling tea leaves with water, milk, sugar, and spices. Before being served, it is strained to remove the tea leaves. Spiced tea is also popular, as are soft drinks.

Throughout India, many small servings of foods are served as appetizers or as snacks. Examples include **samosas** (a deep-fried turnover stuffed with meat, potatoes, or vegetables) and spiced fish balls.

Indians love sweets as snacks or at the end of a meal. Indians make their own version of puddings (almonds may be used to flavor them) and ice cream (in flavors like mango or pistachio!).

For breakfast, the Indian bread chapatis may be cut up, fried in oil, and mixed with yogurt and seasonings. In southern India, steamed rice cakes or rice pancakes may be served instead of chapatis. In some homes, breakfast is made by reheating leftover bread and rice.

At Indian meals, all foods are served at once, even sweets! A typical lunch or dinner includes vegetable dishes; a lentil, bean, or pea dish (or a meat or fish dish, if the family is not vegetarian); rice or bread; and chutneys, raitas, and relishes. Fruit is often served as dessert and also as a break from the spicy foods. Lunch is often delivered from home to people who are working. Foods are served in small bowls. Indians eat with their fingers, scooping their food up with bread.

Vegetables are an important part of the diet in India. Have you ever wondered what happens to vegetables when they're picked? Try the following experiment to learn more!

DO VEGETABLES DIE WHEN YOU PICK THEM?

Materials

2 whole fresh carrots with leaves
knife
cutting board
2 plastic bags
peeler

Purpose

To determine whether freshly picked vegetables are still living.

Procedure

1. Using a knife on a cutting board, cut off the top leaves of one of the carrots.

2. Put each carrot in its own plastic bag and close the bag. Punch several small air holes in each bag.

3. Store the carrots in a refrigerator for 1 week.

4. After 1 week, remove the carrots from their bags. Peel each carrot, then take a bite of each. Which carrot tastes better? Which carrot looks better?

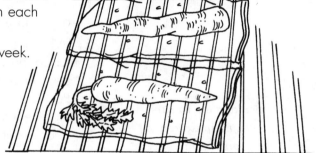

What Happened?

The carrot without the leaves tastes and looks better. Freshly picked vegetables are still living. Carrots are root vegetables, meaning that the carrot is actually the root of the plant. When the leaves (also called carrot tops) are left on carrots, nutrients and water from the carrot continue to feed the leaves of the plant. The carrot itself is less sweet, less tasty, and drier than a carrot with its top removed. If you buy carrots with tops at the store, be sure to remove the tops before you put the carrots in the refrigerator.

The next recipe uses frozen baby carrots, which come with the tops already removed. Remember to serve all of the recipes in this chapter at the same time, the way meals are actually served in India.

Carrots with Grated Coconut and Raisins

Time
30 minutes

Tools
2-cup (480-ml) glass measuring cup

2-quart (2-L) saucepan with lid

steamer basket

medium frying pan

Makes
4 servings

• • • • •
Soaking the raisins makes them extra juicy and plump.
• • • • •

Coconut and raisins frequently accompany meals in India.

Ingredients

½ cup (120 ml) raisins

⅔ pound (300 g) frozen baby carrots

¼ cup (60 ml) margarine

¼ cup (60 ml) honey

¼ cup (60 ml) shredded coconut

Steps

1. Put the raisins in a 2-cup (480-ml) glass measuring cup and add enough hot tap water to cover raisins.

2. While the raisins are soaking, fill a 2-quart (2-L) saucepan with 1 inch (2.5 cm) of water. Place a steamer basket in the saucepan and add the carrots. Put the lid on the saucepan and steam the carrots over high heat for about 15 minutes or until tender when pricked with a fork.

3. When the carrots are almost ready, melt the margarine and honey over medium heat in a medium frying pan.

4. Add the raisins and carrots to the honey mixture and heat through.

5. Serve the carrots topped with shredded coconut.

Lentil and Noodle Soup

Lentils, as well as dried beans and peas, are quite popular in India in both soups and stews. This recipe uses two American substitutes for ingredients used in India: elbow macaroni instead of potatoes, and cheddar cheese instead of Indian cheese.

Time
30 minutes

Tools
large saucepan
knife
cutting board
colander
medium frying pan

Makes
6 servings

Ingredients

½ pound (225 g) elbow macaroni

1 celery stalk

1 medium onion

1 clove garlic

1 tablespoon (15 ml) olive oil

2 cans (19 oz or 538 g) Progresso Lentil Soup

½ cup (120 ml) shredded cheddar cheese

Steps

1. Cook the macaroni in a large saucepan according to the directions on the box (usually about 8 minutes).

2. While the macaroni cooks, wash the celery, then trim the leaves and end off, using a knife on a cutting board.

3. Remove the outer, papery skin of the onion and garlic.

4. Chop the celery, onion, and garlic.

5. When the macaroni is done, drain off the cooking water, using a colander in the sink. Put the macaroni back in the pan.

6. Put the oil in a medium frying pan and heat on medium for 2 minutes.

7. Sauté the celery, onion, and garlic in the oil until tender.

8. Add the sautéed celery, onions, and garlic to the macaroni. Toss.

9. Add the lentil soup and simmer until soup is hot.

10. Serve immediately, garnishing each serving with shredded cheddar cheese.

Baked Fish Topped with Coconut-Tomato Chutney

Time
35 to 45 minutes
to prepare
plus
30 to 40 minutes to bake

Tools
knife

cutting board

grater

medium frying pan

small frying pan

baking dish

Makes
4 servings

This dish is popular in the coastal city of Bombay, where fish and coconuts are plentiful. Normally the fish and chutney are covered and baked in banana leaves. In this recipe, you may substitute cabbage leaves. To save time, you can make the chutney ahead of time and refrigerate it.

Ingredients

3   cloves garlic

1   piece fresh ginger

1   lemon

1   tablespoon (15 ml) vegetable oil

1   teaspoon (5 ml) cinnamon

¼   teaspoon (2 ml) ground cloves

3   cups (720 ml) chopped tomatoes

1   cup (240 ml) shredded coconut

½   cup (120 ml) currants

3   tablespoons (45 ml) honey

2   tablespoons (30 ml) cider vinegar

¼   teaspoon (2 ml) salt

1   pound (450 g) white-fleshed fish fillets

4   large cabbage leaves, washed

4   tablespoons (60 ml) margarine

1   tablespoon (15 ml) lime juice

vegetable oil cooking spray

2   cups (480 ml) cooked rice (optional)

Steps

1. Peel the garlic. Using a knife on a cutting board, mince the garlic.

2. Using your hands, peel the skin off the piece of ginger. Using the smallest holes on a grater, grate the ginger until you have 2 teaspoons (10 ml).

3. Grate part of the yellow rind of the lemon until you have 1 teaspoon (5 ml).

4. Put the oil in a medium frying pan and heat on medium for 2 minutes.

5. Sauté the garlic, ginger, lemon, cinnamon, and cloves in the oil for 2 to 3 minutes, stirring constantly.

6. Add the tomatoes, coconut, currants, honey, cider vinegar, and salt. This is chutney.

7. Simmer until the chutney is thick, about 20 minutes.

8. Preheat oven to 350°F (175°C).

9. Rinse the fish and pat dry. Using a knife on a cutting board, cut the fish into 4 serving-size pieces.

10. Wash the cabbage leaves and dry well.

11. Place a piece of fish at the bottom end of each large cabbage leaf. Put about 2 table-spoons (30 ml) of chutney on each piece of fish. Fold the top end of the cabbage leaf over the fish, tucking the edges under the fish.

12. Melt the margarine over medium heat in a small frying pan.

13. Add the lime juice and stir.

14. Away from any heat, spray a baking dish with vegetable oil cooking spray. Place the fish in the pan. Drizzle the fish with the margarine and lime juice.

15. Bake for 30 to 40 minutes.

16. Serve with rice if desired.

• • • • •
At this point, you can
refrigerate the chutney.
It will keep for 2 weeks.
• • • • •

Chapatis

Time
1 hour 15 minutes
to prepare
plus
overnight to refrigerate
plus
30 minutes to cook

Tools
large mixing bowl

plastic wrap

waxed paper

cookie sheet

medium frying pan
or large skillet
or griddle

metal spatula

Makes
12 chapatis

Chapatis are a popular Indian flatbread eaten at most meals. Try the following recipe to make your own chapatis.

Ingredients

2 cups (480 ml) whole wheat flour

1 teaspoon (5 ml) salt

⅔ to ¾ cup (160 to 180 ml) warm water

2 tablespoons (30 ml) all-purpose flour

Steps

1. In a large mixing bowl, use your hands to mix together the flour and salt.

2. Add the water a little at a time just until the dough no longer sticks in clumps to your hands or the bowl. Add a few more drops of water if needed.

3. Transfer the dough to a flat surface and knead the dough until it is smooth, about 5 minutes.

4. Wrap the dough in plastic wrap and allow it to rest for 45 minutes.

5. Divide the dough into 12 pieces. To do this, first divide the dough in half, then divide each piece in half again to make 4 pieces. Then divide each piece into 3 pieces.

6. Roll each piece into a ball. Flatten the ball with your palms to make a 4- to 5-inch (10- to 12.5-cm) circle.

7. Stack the chapatis by putting waxed paper between them and placing the stacks on a cookie sheet. Cover with plastic wrap and refrigerate overnight.

8. Preheat a medium frying pan, large skillet, or griddle, by placing it on a burner and setting the heat to medium for 2 minutes.

9. Place as many chapatis as you can on the ungreased cooking surface.

10. Cook on low to medium heat for 1 minute. Press each chapati with a metal spatula and let cook about 1 minute longer or until browned on the bottom.

11. Turn the chapatis and cook the other side as in step 10.

Mango with Yogurt Dressing

Time
15 minutes

Tools
paring knife

cutting board

4 individual serving bowls

Makes
4 servings

A **mango** is an oval or round fruit weighing from 1 to 5 pounds (0.5 to 2.3 kg) that Indians have grown for thousands of years. Its skin is usually green but can be yellow or red. The fruit inside is golden and tastes sweet. A mango is ripe when it feels soft to the touch, but not too soft. Once ripe, it should be stored in the refrigerator. This mango dessert is served with plain yogurt topped with pistachio nuts, a favorite Indian nut.

Ingredients

1 large ripe mango

1 cup (240 ml) plain nonfat or low-fat yogurt

2 tablespoons (30 ml) chopped pistachios

Steps

1. Using a paring knife, peel the mango. It will be juicy.

2. Using a knife on a cutting board, cut the mango into bite-sized pieces. Avoid cutting around the mango's pit, where the fruit is tough.

3. Put an equal amount of mango pieces in each of 4 individual serving bowls.

4. Put ¼ cup (60 ml) of plain yogurt and ½ tablespoon (8 ml) of chopped pistachios on top of each serving.

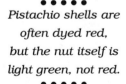

• • • • •
Pistachio shells are often dyed red, but the nut itself is light green, not red.
• • • • •

CHAPTER 10
CHINA

China is the most populated country on earth! It is bordered by many countries, including Russia, North Korea, and India. China includes 22 provinces and 5 autonomous regions.

There is no single Chinese cooking style. Instead there are a number of regional styles. Four important regions are northern (the area around Peking), coastal, western, and southern (the area around Canton) China.

In the northern region, the staple food is wheat flour, not rice. Wheat is used to make many noodle dishes and dumplings. The northern region is well known for sweet-and-sour dishes and Peking duck.

Rice is a staple along coastal China. The coastal region uses much fish and shellfish from the East China Sea and its many rivers. Eastern Chinese dishes often use a large variety of vegetables, because this area is quite fertile and has a year-round growing season.

Western China is famous for Szechwan pepper. This pepper, from the southwestern province of Szechwan, is strong and hot, unlike black pepper. Western Chinese cuisine is known for its spiciness.

From Canton in southern China come **egg rolls,** wheat dough that has been filled with meat and vegetables, then fried. Southern China is also famous for stir-fried foods and **dim sum,** steamed dumplings stuffed with meat or seafood.

Stir-frying is the most common method of cooking Chinese food. Stir-frying involves cooking bite-sized pieces of food over medium-high heat in a small amount of oil (usually soybean oil) while stirring constantly. Moving the foods around in the pan ensures that they cook evenly and quickly over high heat. Stir-frying rarely takes more than five minutes. Chicken and vegetables are a favorite for stir-frying. A **wok** (rhymes with sock) is an all-purpose Chinese pan that is commonly used for stir-frying because its even heat allows quick cooking. A wok looks like a wide cone that is rounded at the bottom. Food is easily turned along its sloping sides. In addition to its use for stir-frying, a wok can be used to steam or deep-fry foods.

Vegetables, rice and other grains, and foods made from soybeans are probably the most important foods in China. Plain rice is served at all meals. Sometimes fried rice is served. Fried rice is made by adding egg to plain rice and stir-frying it.

In one form or another, soybeans are found at every meal. Milk made from soybeans, called soy milk, is drunk like cow's milk. Soybean sprouts are common. **Tofu,** a cheeselike food made from soybeans, is used in many main dishes. Soy sauce is also made from soybeans.

Meat is a luxury. Fish and shellfish are more common, but pork and poultry are sometimes consumed. Popular fish include pike, carp, and bass.

Some interesting fruits and vegetables used in China include the following:

- Bamboo shoots are sprouts of young bamboo grass.

- Chinese cabbage, also called **bok choy,** is a vegetable with long white stalks and green leaves.
- Snow peas have thin, flat pods that are edible.
- Water chestnuts are the delicately flavored fruit of a long-stemmed water plant.
- **Kumquats** are a small fruit that resemble oranges but are not citrus fruit. The skin of the kumquat is sweet, but the inside is sour.
- **Litchis** are a round, red fruit with a raisinlike flavor that can be eaten alone or with other fruits.

Common spices are cinnamon, cloves, Szechwan pepper, and sesame seeds.

The Chinese do not have any foods that are specifically for breakfast, lunch, or dinner. Rice, noodles, vegetables, beans, fish, poultry, and meat are eaten at any meal.

A typical Chinese meal has no main dish. Instead there are several side dishes and rice, noodles, or pancakes. Soup may also be served. Examples of side dishes include stir-fried chicken with snow peas, shrimp with **hoisin sauce** (a dark, sweet sauce made from soybeans, sugar, and spices), bean sprouts with scallions, and Chinese cabbage. The Chinese eat a mouthful of rice and then a mouthful of a side dish, continuing on like this throughout the meal. In China, people serve themselves at the table from platters of food put in the center. Each person has

a bowl for rice, a bowl for the other foods, a tiny saucer for bones, and chopsticks.

Tea, the main beverage, plays an important role in the life of the Chinese. People drink it anytime and anywhere. It is always drunk black—without cream, milk, sugar, or lemon.

Dessert is always fruit, except on special occasions. The fortune cookies that are served at many Chinese restaurants in the United States are not truly Chinese. Almond cookies, however, are an authentic Chinese sweet. Another sweet Chinese dessert is a fruit float flavored with almond extract. Try the following experiment to understand the science behind orange soda, the main ingredient in an orange float.

EXPERIMENT

WHAT MAKES ORANGE SODA FIZZ?

Purpose

To understand what happens when you mix an acid with a base.

Materials

1 cup (240 ml) water
½ cup (120 ml) vinegar
1 cup (240 ml) orange juice
3 bowls
3 teaspoons (15 ml) baking soda

Procedure

1. Pour the water, vinegar, and orange juice into 3 separate bowls.

2. Place 1 teaspoon (5 ml) of baking soda in each of the 3 bowls.

3. Which liquids have bubbles in them?

What Happened?

The vinegar and the orange juice became bubbly, but nothing happened to the water. This is because vinegar and orange juice are acids, and baking soda, or **bicarbonate of soda,** is a base. You learned about acids and bases in Chapter 6. As you know, they are chemicals with certain properties. One of the properties is that a chemical reaction occurs when acids and bases are put together. A **chemical reaction** is the breaking apart of substances to make new substances. When baking soda, a base, is combined with the acid vinegar or orange juice, a new substance, a gas called **carbon dioxide,** is made. The fizzing and bubbles you see are the carbon dioxide being released. No bubbles or fizzing occur when baking soda is combined with water, because water is neither an acid nor a base.

In this experiment, adding baking soda to orange juice makes bubbles of carbon dioxide like those in orange soda or any other soft drink. **But don't drink your experiment—it isn't orange soda!** Use orange soda from a can or bottle for the next recipe, Bubbly Mandarin Orange–Pineapple Float. Serve with Chopstick-Friendly Chicken and Veggie Stir-Fry, Awesome Egg Rolls, and Incredible Almond Cookies.

Bubbly Mandarin Orange–Pineapple Float

Time
10 minutes

Tools
can opener

colander

blender

4 tall glasses

ice cream scoop

4 spoons

4 straws

Makes
4 servings

This recipe uses mandarin oranges, a fruit grown on certain Chinese orange trees.

Ingredients

11-ounce (312-g) can mandarin oranges

8-ounce (225-g) can crushed pineapple

3 scoops orange sherbet

1 cup (240 ml) orange soda

4 ice cubes

4 scoops vanilla ice cream

Steps

1. Open the cans of mandarin oranges and crushed pineapple. Then empty the cans into a colander to drain off the liquid.

2. Put the mandarin oranges, crushed pineapple, orange sherbet, orange soda, and ice cubes in a blender.

3. Put the lid on and blend at high speed until foamy and smooth.

4. Pour into tall glasses. Float a scoop of vanilla ice cream in each drink. Serve with a spoon and a straw.

Chopstick-Friendly Chicken and Veggie Stir-Fry

When you stir-fry, use a large, heavy skillet or a wok, and add a small amount of oil or use a vegetable cooking spray. The food should be cooked at medium-high heat. Because stir-frying is such a quick cooking process at high heat, it is a good idea to line up your ingredients next to the skillet before you begin cooking.

Time
35 minutes

Tools
knife

cutting board

grater

wok *or* heavy skillet

small bowl

Makes
6 servings

Ingredients

2 stalks celery

3 scallions

8 mushrooms

1 red pepper

2 cloves garlic

1 piece fresh ginger

2 boneless chicken breasts

1 tablespoon (15 ml) peanut oil

1 cup (240 ml) frozen snow pea pods, thawed

¼ cup (60 ml) water chestnuts

1 cup (240 ml) chicken broth

2 tablespoons (30 ml) soy sauce

2 tablespoons (30 ml) cornstarch

2 tablespoons (30 ml) cold water

8-ounce (225-g) can pineapple chunks, drained

3 cups (700 ml) rice, cooked

Steps

1. Wash the celery, scallions, mushrooms, and red pepper.

2. Using a knife on a cutting board, cut off the leaves and ends of the celery, the roots and wilted leaf ends of the scallions, and the stems of the mushrooms.

3. Slice the celery diagonally. Cut the scallions and mushrooms into ¼-inch (6-mm) slices.

4. Cut the pepper in half. Remove and discard the seeds and ribs. Cut the pepper into strips, then dice.

5. Peel and mince the garlic.

To use chopsticks, hold one in the crook of your thumb and grasp it between your thumb joint and middle finger. Hold the other much like a pencil, grasping it between your thumb pad and index (pointer) finger. Keep the first chopstick still while moving the other to pick up pieces of food.

6. Using your hands, peel the skin off the piece of ginger. Using the smallest holes on a grater, grate the ginger until you have 1 tablespoon (15 ml).

7. Rinse the chicken breasts in cold running water and pat dry. Using a knife on a cutting board, cut chicken into thin strips about ½ inch (13 mm) wide and 2 inches (50 mm) long.

8. In a wok or heavy skillet, heat the peanut oil over medium-high heat. Add the chicken and stir-fry for 2 to 3 minutes.

9. Add the celery, scallions, mushrooms, and peppers. Stir-fry for 2 to 3 minutes.

10. Add the snow peas and water chestnuts. Stir-fry for 2 to 3 minutes or until all vegetables are tender crisp.

11. Add the chicken broth and soy sauce to the stir-fry. Bring to a boil by covering for about 2 minutes.

12. While waiting for the stir-fry to boil, mix the cornstarch and cold water in a small bowl until smooth.

13. Add the cornstarch mixture slowly to the stir-fry, stirring constantly. Cook stir-fry until thickened and vegetables are coated with a thin glaze.

14. Stir in the pineapple chunks.

15. Serve over rice and eat with chopsticks.

• • • • •
When stir-frying, remember to keep the food moving around the wok to cook it completely and evenly.
• • • • •

• • • • •
Cornstarch acts to thicken foods, but it must first be mixed with a cold liquid to work correctly.
• • • • •

Egg roll dough is made simply of flour, water, and salt. This dough is filled with meat or seafood and oodles of chopped vegetables. For convenience, use ready-made egg roll wrappers, which can be purchased in the frozen section of the supermarket or a Chinese food specialty store. Egg rolls are fried in fat. To do this safely, you will need a Dutch oven, which is a very large pot that usually has handles.

Ingredients

1 stalk celery

2 scallions

½ cup (120 ml) water chestnuts

1¼ cups (300 ml) cooked baby shrimp

½ pound (227 g) ground turkey

1 tablespoon (15 ml) soy sauce

½ teaspoon (3 ml) cornstarch

1 teaspoon (5 ml) cold water

6 frozen egg roll wrappers, thawed

1 egg

1 teaspoon (5 ml) water

vegetable oil

Time
20 minutes to prepare
plus
15 minutes to cook

Tools
knife

cutting board

medium bowl

measuring cup

plate

paper towels

small bowl

pastry brush

Dutch oven

Makes
6 egg rolls

Steps

1. Wash the celery and scallions.

2. Using a knife on a cutting board, cut off the leaves and the end of the celery and the roots and wilted leaf ends of the scallions. Slice the celery and scallions, then chop.

3. Chop enough water chestnuts to make ⅓ cup (80 ml).

4. Rinse the baby shrimp under cold running water and pat dry. Chop.

5. In a medium bowl, mix together the celery, scallions, water chestnuts, baby shrimp, ground turkey, and soy sauce.

6. In a measuring cup, mix the cornstarch with the cold water, then add to the medium bowl. Stir. This is the filling for the egg rolls.

7. Put the egg roll wrappers on a plate and cover with a damp paper towel so that they don't dry out.

8. In a small bowl, beat 1 egg and 1 teaspoon (5 ml) water. This is called egg wash.

9. Place one egg roll wrapper on a cutting board, turning the wrapper so that it is diamond-shaped.

10. Place 1 heaping tablespoon (15 ml) of the filling in the center of the egg roll. Using a pastry brush, brush egg wash over the four corners of the egg roll wrapper.

11. Fold three sides of the egg roll wrapper so that the egg roll looks like an envelope with its top flap open. Roll up the egg roll.

12. Repeat steps 9 to 11 to make the remaining 5 egg rolls.

13. In a large Dutch oven, heat 1 inch (2.5 cm) of oil to 375°F (190°C).

14. Fry the egg rolls about 15 minutes, turning occasionally, until deep golden brown.

15. Drain and cool on paper towels.

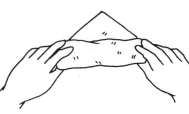

Incredible Almond Cookies

Fortune cookies are not really Chinese, but these almond cookies are! Try them with Chinese ginger ice cream!

Time
15 minutes to prepare
plus
35 to 40 minutes to bake

Tools
medium bowl
2 table knives
cutting board
pastry blender
small bowl
cookie sheet

Makes
24 cookies

Ingredients

2¾ cups (660 ml) all-purpose flour

1 cup (240 ml) sugar

1½ teaspoon (3 ml) baking soda

¼ teaspoon (1 ml) salt

1 cup (240 ml) butter

2 eggs

1 tablespoon (15 ml) almond extract

1 egg white

1 teaspoon (5 ml) water

24 whole almonds

Steps

1. Preheat the oven to 325°F (160°C).

2. Put the flour, sugar, baking soda, and salt in a medium bowl. Mix well.

3. Using a table knife on a cutting board, cut the butter into small pieces. Put the butter in the bowl with the flour mixture.

4. Cut in the butter with a pastry blender, *or*, holding a table knife in each hand, draw the knives across each other to cut through the butter and dry ingredients. Keep cutting in until the mixture is in pieces about the size of small peas.

5. Stir in 2 eggs and the almond extract.

6. With your hands, roll pieces of dough into 1-inch (25-mm) balls. Flour your hands lightly if the dough sticks to your fingers.

7. Place the cookies 2 inches (5 cm) apart on an ungreased cookie sheet.

8. In a small bowl, beat the egg white and 1 teaspoon (5 ml) water to make egg wash.

9. Press an almond into the center of each cookie, then lightly brush each cookie with egg wash.

10. Bake in batches for 15 to 20 minutes per batch or until the bottom is lightly browned.

CHAPTER 11

JAPAN

Japan, one of the world's most populous countries, is a chain of islands along Asia's east coast. Its four major islands span 1,200 miles (1,900 km). The country of Japan also includes over 3,900 smaller islands. Japan is surrounded by the Pacific Ocean, the Sea of Japan, and the East China Sea.

HOKKAIDO

Sea of Japan

JAPAN
HONSHU

Tokyo

Pacific Ocean

Osaka

SHIKOKU

KYUSHU

East China Sea

Some people are surprised to learn that Japanese food is quite different in appearance and taste from Chinese food. While Chinese food is often stir-fried, the Japanese like to simmer, boil, steam, or broil their foods. When the Japanese do fry, as in **tempura** dishes, the food is first coated with batter before it is deep-fried. Also, Japanese foods are not as highly seasoned as Chinese dishes.

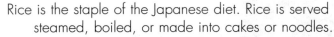

Rice is the staple of the Japanese diet. Rice is served steamed, boiled, or made into cakes or noodles. Japanese cuisine also relies on a variety of noodles, made from wheat, buckwheat, or mung beans. Noodles may be served hot or cold, with meals or as a snack.

As in Chinese cooking, soybean products are important. These include tofu, **miso** (soybean paste), soybean sprouts, and soy sauce. Tofu is sautéed, boiled, broiled, used to garnish soups, or scrambled with eggs. Japanese soy sauce, or **shoyu** (SHOH-yoo), is generally lighter and more delicately flavored than Chinese soy sauce. Soy sauce is made from soybeans, roasted wheat or barley, salt, water, and malt. The Japanese, like the Chinese who invented soy sauce, use it as a dip, as a seasoning for cooking liquids, and as an ingredient in marinades.

As can easily be imagined, seafood is a star ingredient of this country made up of islands. Seafood is also important because, until the nineteenth century, many Japanese followed Buddhist teachings that included eating seafood along with a vegetarian diet. In addition to seafood, Japanese today do eat meat and poultry. Beef is not an important part of the Japanese diet, largely because it is so expensive.

Japanese cooks keep the seasons in mind when planning their menus. This is done to ensure that they use fruits and vegetables that are in season. Watercress, for example, is a spring vegetable. Summer vegetables are plentiful and include beans, peas, lettuce, tomatoes, and cucumbers. Carrots and turnips are a part of many winter meals, as is **daikon** (DYE-kahn), a giant white radish that is tender and can be eaten raw. A popular winter fruit is the tangerine, a variety of mandarin orange grown in Japan.

Typical seasonings include the following:

- **Rice wine vinegar** is made from rice wine.

- **Wasabi** is a green Japanese radish with a strong flavor.
- Sesame oil is a very flavorful oil made from roasted sesame seeds.
- Ginger is a bumpy root that gives a hot, spicy flavor to foods.
- **Yakitori** is a classic Japanese flavoring that combines soy sauce, rice wine, and sugar. It is often used for broiled or grilled dishes.

The classic Japanese breakfast is a bowl of rice with **nori,** a type of seaweed that is dried in sheets and crumbled over the rice, and a soup called **misoshiru** (mee-soh-SHIH-roo) that is made with miso, tofu, seaweed, and vegetables. Western-style breakfasts, including bread, eggs, and pancakes, are becoming more popular.

A Japanese lunch or dinner consists of many side dishes served at the same time. The dishes are usually prepared in different ways, such as fried and steamed, or they have different tastes, such as sweet and spicy. One of the dishes is usually a salad. Salad dressings are often thick and use tofu or miso as their main ingredient. Some salads are made with vinegar dressings.

Lunch is generally light and may include seafood or vegetables cooked in soy sauce with rice or noodles. The evening meal is the most important meal. Soup usually starts the meal. Then several small dishes are served, along with rice and salad.

Tea is drunk during and after meals. Loose green tea is the most popular. Tea is always taken without milk, sugar, or lemon.

At mealtime, Japanese families sit on cushions around a low table. Instead of using forks, knives, or spoons, the Japanese use chopsticks.

Part of the art of Japanese cooking has to do with presenting the food attractively. Food is very carefully arranged on dishes. Simple arrangements are preferred.

You'll find broccoli as a main ingredient in many Japanese dishes, such as tempura. Try the following experiment to see what happens when broccoli is cooked with lemon juice or baking soda.

EXPERIMENT

WHAT HAPPENS WHEN YOU COOK BROCCOLI IN AN ACID OR A BASE?

Purpose

To study the chemical reactions that occur when a vegetable is cooked with an acid or a base.

Materials

3 cups (720 ml) water

3 small saucepans

1½ cups (360 ml) frozen broccoli florets

1 tablespoon (15 ml) lemon juice

1 teaspoon (5 ml) baking soda

fork

Procedure

1. Place 1 cup (240 ml) of water in each of the saucepans.

2. Add ½ cup (120 ml) of frozen broccoli to each pan. Bring each pan to a boil, then lower the heat to simmer.

3. Add 1 tablespoon (15 ml) of lemon juice to one saucepan and 1 teaspoon (5 ml) of baking soda to the second. Do nothing to the third pan.

4. Let the broccoli cook for 8 minutes.

5. What color is the broccoli in each pan? Use a fork to test the tenderness of the broccoli in each pan. Which pan has the mushiest broccoli?

What Happened?

The broccoli cooked in lemon juice, an acid, is an ugly olive-green color. The broccoli cooked in baking soda, a base, is bright green in color and clearly the mushiest! The plain broccoli is close to its natural color.

Green vegetables are rich in **chlorophyll,** the green pigment of plants. When an acid such as lemon juice is added to the cooking water of green vegetables, a chemical reaction occurs between the chlorophyll and the acid, causing the broccoli to turn a drab olive-green color. (The broccoli will also turn this color if it is overcooked.) When a base such as baking soda is added, green vegetables stay green but become mushy. Baking soda destroys the cell walls of the plant, so the vegetable becomes too soft and slippery to eat. No chemical reaction occurs when broccoli is cooked for a short time in boiling water, as water is neither an acid nor a base.

As you can probably guess, the Japanese don't cook their broccoli with lemon juice or baking soda! Use fresh broccoli in the next recipe, Steamed Broccoli with Sesame Seed Dressing. Serve it with Fast 'n' Easy Beef Teriyaki and Japanese Soba Noodles in Broth for an authentic Japanese dinner.

Steamed Broccoli with Sesame Seed Dressing

Time
20 minutes

Tools
knife

cutting board

colander

2-quart (2-L) saucepan
with lid

steamer basket

small frying pan

Makes
4 servings

The Japanese usually eat this dish cold. For something different, you can use another vegetable, such as snow peas, instead of broccoli.

Ingredients

1 pound (454 g) broccoli

2 tablespoons (30 ml) sesame seeds

2 tablespoons (30 ml) soy sauce

1 tablespoon (15 ml) brown sugar

Steps

1. Using a knife on a cutting board, cut the florets off the broccoli, leaving only about 1 inch (25 mm) of stalk on each floret.

2. Put the broccoli florets into a colander and rinse well under cold running water.

3. Fill a 2-quart (2-L) saucepan with 1 inch (2.5 cm) of water. Place a steamer basket in the saucepan and add the broccoli. Put the lid on the saucepan and steam the broccoli over high heat for about 6 to 9 minutes or until tender when pricked with a fork.

4. When the broccoli is almost ready, cook the sesame seeds, soy sauce, and brown sugar over medium heat in a small frying pan for 2 to 3 minutes.

5. Put the broccoli in a serving dish and drizzle the soy sauce mixture over it. Serve immediately.

Fast 'n' Easy Beef Teriyaki

Teriyaki describes the process by which meat or seafood is broiled with a sauce. The word teriyaki *translates as "shining broil." Broiling turns the sauce into a shiny, glazed coating. When broiling the meat, make sure an adult is in the kitchen with you.*

Time
15 minutes to prepare
plus
1 hour to marinate
plus
20 minutes to cook

Tools
knife

cutting board

grater

medium bowl

wire whip

shallow baking dish

broiler pan

oven mitts

spoon

Makes
4 servings

Ingredients

2 cloves garlic

1 large piece fresh ginger

¾ cup (180 ml) soy sauce

2 tablespoons (30 ml) Worcestershire sauce

¼ cup (60 ml) dark brown sugar, packed

2 tablespoons (30 ml) lemon juice

1 pound (454 g) boneless sirloin or flank steak, 1 inch (2.5 cm) thick

Steps

1. Peel the garlic. Using a knife on a cutting board, mince the garlic.

2. Using your hands, peel the skin off the piece of ginger. Using the smallest holes on a grater, grate the ginger until you have 2 tablespoons (30 ml).

3. In a medium bowl, whisk together the garlic, ginger, soy sauce, Worcestershire sauce, brown sugar, and lemon juice.

4. Place the steak in a shallow baking pan and pour the soy sauce marinade over it.

5. Let the meat marinate at room temperature for 1 hour.

6. Preheat the broiler.

7. Transfer the meat from the marinade to a broiler pan. Spoon some of the marinade over the steak.

• • • • •
The soy sauce marinade will flavor and soften the meat.
• • • • •

8. Placing the broiler pan about 3 to 4 inches from the heat, broil the meat for 7 to 10 minutes. *Keep an eye on the meat at all times to make sure it does not over-cook!*

9. Using oven mitts, slide the oven rack out. Turn the meat over and spoon more marinade over the steak. Broil for about 10 minutes longer.

10. Remove the steak and slice it. Serve immediately.

Japanese Soba Noodles in Broth

Time
30 minutes

Soba noodles are flat, thin, brownish gray noodles made from buckwheat flour. Look for them at Asian food stores and many natural food stores if you can't find them at your supermarket. They are often served cold or warm in a fish broth. In this recipe, soba noodles are served in chicken broth.

Tools
large saucepan

small saucepan

colander

4 individual serving bowls

Makes
4 servings

Ingredients

½ pound (227 g) soba noodles

24-ounce (680-g) can low-sodium chicken broth

2 teaspoons (10 ml) dried parsley flakes

Steps

1. Fill a large saucepan two-thirds full with water. Bring to a boil over high heat.

2. Add the noodles. When the water boils again, reduce the heat to medium. Cook for about 20 minutes or until tender.

3. When the noodles are almost ready, put the chicken broth and dried parsley flakes in a small saucepan. Bring to a boil over medium-high heat.

4. Drain the noodles in a colander.

5. Spoon the noodles into 4 individual serving bowls.

6. Put some broth in each bowl and serve immediately.

 THAILAND

The kingdom of Thailand is in the center of mainland southeastern Asia. Its coastal area is on the Gulf of Thailand. Due to the country's central location, Thai cooking has been influenced by other cultures. From the Chinese, Thai cooks learned how to stir-fry foods. From the Indians, they learned how to use a combination of spices to flavor dishes.

Within Thailand, each region has developed its own style of cooking. For instance, curries are popular in southern Thailand, where chilis are included in every meal. Fresh seafood is especially popular on the southern peninsula. The Thai on the central plain like spicy foods, while their neighbors to the north prefer milder dishes. Grilled foods with rich sauces are favorites in northeastern Thailand.

Rice is eaten with almost every meal. Noodles made from rice, eggs, or mung beans are also a regular part of Thai meals.

Seafood from the Gulf of Thailand and its rivers is an important part of Thai cooking. Popular seafood includes mussels, crabs, lobsters, scallops, shrimp, and fish of all varieties. Favorite dishes include steamed fish served with vegetable salads made with small amounts of beef.

Herbs, spices, and sauces play an important role in cooking. The Thai particularly like sweet, sour, and salty tastes. Popular flavorings include black pepper, curry powder, basil, coriander, fresh ginger, garlic, lemon juice, oyster sauce, and soy sauce. Lemon grass, a tropical grass that has an edible lower, white part, is also used to flavor foods. At most meals, the Thai use a special sauce, called **nam pla prig,** made from fish sauce, garlic, red peppers, and lemon juice.

Popular fruit includes bananas, pineapples, papayas, coconuts, and mangoes. **Rambutans** (red, oval-shaped fruit) and **shaddocks** (similar to grapefruit) are native to Thailand. Popular vegetables include collard greens, green beans, bell peppers, scallions, and bean sprouts.

Sweet dishes in Thailand often use bananas, rice, coconut milk, and sugar as ingredients. Two examples are stewed bananas with coconut milk and coconut custard.

Breakfast in Thailand is often leftovers from yesterday's dinner and rice. A typical lunch consists of noodles with stir-fried vegetables. Dinner is a heavier meal, usually a fresh salad, soup or a curry dish, a dip or sauce, rice, and various dishes featuring meat, chicken, seafood, and stir-fried vegetables. For all Thai meals, the appearance of the foods on the plate is very important. Time is taken to present food in an artistic manner.

Bean sprouts are frequently found in Thai dishes. Try the following experiment to learn where bean sprouts come from.

HOW DO BEAN SPROUTS GROW?

Materials

4 tablespoons (60 ml) dry mung beans (or lentils, if mung beans are not available)

medium bowl

colander

2 medium drinking glasses

2 small pieces cheesecloth

2 rubber bands

Purpose

To understand how bean sprouts grow.

Procedure

1. Wash the beans and remove any foreign materials.
2. Soak them overnight in a medium bowl filled with warm water.
3. Using a colander, drain off the soaking water. Divide the beans equally between the 2 glasses.
4. Put a piece of cheesecloth on top of each glass to cover it. Secure the cheesecloth with a rubber band around the top of the glass.
5. Put one glass in the refrigerator and the other glass in a warm, dark place, such as a cabinet.
6. Twice a day, rinse the beans in each glass with luke-warm water. Drain excess water through the cheese-cloth so that the beans don't get moldy.
7. After 4 days, observe the glasses. Which batch of beans sprouted?

What Happened?

The beans that were put into the warm, dark place sprouted and produced quite a few bean sprouts. Inside each bean is an **embryo,** a seed from which a new plant will grow when given water, warmth, and darkness. You provided the beans with water when you soaked them overnight. The water entered the beans, and the starches in the beans absorbed the water and swelled.

In addition to water, you provided one of the glasses with warmth and darkness, which allowed the beans to sprout. The cold temperature of the refrigerator prevented the embryos inside the refrigerated beans from growing.

Use your bean sprouts in the Thai Salad recipe. Serve your salad with the Zippy Fried Rice with Chicken and the Banana-Nut Dessert. Remember, the way you present the food on the plate is very important in Thailand, so spend a few extra minutes arranging the foods.

Thai Salad with Bean Sprouts

All kinds of fresh, raw vegetables are used in Thai salads. Salads are always served with the dinner meal.

Time
20 minutes

Tools
8 individual salad bowls

knife

cutting board

medium bowl

Makes
8 servings

Ingredients

1 head Bibb lettuce

10-ounce (283-g) bag fresh spinach

1 small carrot

1 stalk celery

2 scallions

8 cherry tomatoes

½ cup (120 ml) fresh bean sprouts

¼ cup (60 ml) peanut oil

3 tablespoons (45 ml) lime juice

2 tablespoons (30 ml) rice wine vinegar

½ teaspoon (3 ml) cayenne pepper

Steps

1. Wash the lettuce and spinach leaves, removing any damaged leaves and the spinach stems. Pat dry. Arrange in 8 individual salad bowls.

2. Wash the carrot, celery, and scallions. Using a knife on a cutting board, remove the ends of the carrot and celery, and the roots and green part of the scallions. Slice the vegetables thinly.

3. Wash the cherry tomatoes and bean sprouts.

4. Evenly distribute the carrots, celery, scallions, cherry tomatoes, and bean sprouts among the four salads.

5. In a medium bowl, make a salad dressing by whisking the oil, lime juice, vinegar, and cayenne pepper.

6. Drizzle the dressing over the salads and serve immediately.

• • • • •

Cayenne pepper, like the jalapeño pepper, is very hot. Be careful handling it so that it does not get in your eyes.

• • • • •

Zippy Fried Rice with Chicken

Fried rice came to Thailand from China. The Thai quickly adopted the recipe and made changes to it to suit their eating style. Fried rice is often served at breakfast or lunch. It often contains leftover meats or seafood.

Time
30 minutes

Tools
2-quart (2-L) saucepan with lid

knife

cutting board

grater

large frying pan

Makes
4 servings

Ingredients

1½ cups (360 ml) white rice, uncooked

2 cups water

2 tablespoons (30 ml) soy sauce

1 tablespoon (15 ml) Worcestershire sauce

1 dash Tabasco sauce

1 pinch cayenne pepper

½ teaspoon (3 ml) salt

½ teaspoon (3 ml) ground ginger

¼ teaspoon (2 ml) garlic powder

3 scallions

1 medium carrot

1 teaspoon (5 ml) butter

1 tablespoon (15 ml) vegetable oil

1½ cups (360 ml) cooked chicken, cut into bite-sized pieces

1 cup (240 ml) frozen snow pea pods, thawed

3-ounce (85-g) can sliced mushrooms, drained

¼ cup (60 ml) cashews

⅓ cup (80 ml) raisins

Steps

1. Place the rice, water, soy sauce, Worcestershire sauce, Tabasco sauce, cayenne pepper, and salt in a 2-quart (2-L) saucepan.

2. Add the ginger and garlic powder. Put the lid on and bring to a boil over high heat. Then, reduce the heat to low and simmer for 20 minutes.

3. While the rice is cooking, wash the scallions and carrot.

4. Using a knife on a cutting board, cut off the root ends and green parts of the scallions. Slice the white part of the scallions.

5. Using the smallest holes on a grater, grate the carrot.

6. Put the butter and oil in a large frying pan and heat on medium for 2 minutes or until the butter is melted.

7. Sauté the scallions and carrots in the butter mixture for 2 to 3 minutes.

8. Add the chicken, snow pea pods, and mushrooms. Continue cooking for another 3 to 4 minutes, stirring occasionally.

9. Add the cashews and raisins. Cook for 3 more minutes.

10. When the rice is cooked, stir it into the frying pan. Stir for 2 to 3 minutes. Serve immediately.

Banana-Nut Dessert

Time
15 minutes
plus
2 hours chilling time

Tools
medium bowl

electric mixer

4 individual serving bowls

knife

cutting board

Makes
4 servings

Peanuts were introduced to Thai cooking by Thailand's neighbor, Malaysia. Although Thai cooks do not use instant pudding as in this recipe, they do make custards that are similar, using ingredients such as banana or coconut.

Ingredients

3.4 ounce (96 g) package instant vanilla pudding mix

2 cups (480 ml) skim or low-fat milk

1 banana

12 peanuts

Steps

1. Put the pudding mix and milk in a medium bowl.

2. With an electric mixer, mix at the lowest speed for 1 to 2 minutes.

3. Pour into 4 individual serving bowls and put in the refrigerator to chill for about 2 hours.

4. Using a knife on a cutting board, slice the banana and chop the peanuts.

5. To serve, top the puddings with the banana and nuts.

PART 6

AFRICA

CHAPTER 13

MOROCCO

Morocco is found in northern Africa, bordered by the Sahara desert and the country of Algeria.

Moroccan cuisine features stuffed vegetables, soups, stews, and salads. Many meat dishes include fruit or other sweet foods. For example, chicken is cooked with kumquats. Pork is not eaten because Islam, the major religion, forbids the eating of pork. Meats are often cut into bite-sized chunks and grilled. Wheat is the grain used most often.

Spices and herbs are also important. This is because northern Africa was once part of the spice route between the Far East and Europe. In Morocco, however, foods are more subtly spiced than in neighboring countries. A favorite spice mixture in Morocco, called **ras al hanout** (RAHS-ahl-hah-noo), is made of cinnamon, cumin, coriander, ginger, and turmeric. Another favorite Moroccan spice is saffron, noted for its bright yellow color and exotic taste.

A typical Moroccan meal starts with **b'stilla** (a piece of dough that is stuffed with layers of pigeon meat, spices, and sugar, then fried) followed by couscous. **Couscous** is a dish made with a type of wheat flour that is steamed over a stew of lamb or chicken and vegetables. Spices, such as saffron, are added to couscous.

Dessert in Morocco might be a pudding made with milk, raisins, almonds, and currants, and thickened with semolina. **Criouch** (kree-OOSH), a type of cake covered with honey and sesame seeds, is also common. A popular beverage is minted tea.

Desserts often use honey as a sweetener. Try the following activity to experiment with honey and learn about viscosity.

HOW DOES HONEY FLOW?

Materials

3 small clear drinking glasses of same size
water
honey
4 marbles
pancake syrup

Purpose

To understand the concept of viscosity.

Procedure

1. Fill the first glass with water and the second glass with an equal amount of honey.

2. Hold 1 marble in each hand and place a hand over each glass. Release both marbles at the same time. Watch closely to see which marble reaches the bottom first. Record your observations.

3. Discard the water from the first glass and fill that glass with an equal amount of pancake syrup.

4. Repeat step 2 with the remaining 2 marbles. Compare how quickly the marble falls in the pancake syrup to how quickly it falls in the honey.

What Happened?

The marble in the glass filled with honey took longer to reach the bottom than did the marbles in the glasses filled with water or pancake syrup. This is because honey is more viscous than water or pancake syrup. **Viscosity** is a liquid's resistance to flow. All liquids flow to fill the space that holds them. A very viscous liquid is one that flows slowly. The marble that took longest to fall was in the most viscous liquid. This experiment also showed that honey is more viscous than pancake syrup, both of which are more viscous than water.

Toss out the honey and pancake syrup when you're done with the experiment, but don't put away the honey jar. You'll need it to make delicious Almond and Honey Pastries. Serve this dessert after the hearty Couscous.

•••• Almond and Honey •••• Pastries

In Morocco, pastry dough is made and filled with various ingredients to make a sweet dessert. In this recipe, the pastry dough is covered with almonds and honey.

Ingredients

1 cup (240 ml) slivered almonds

1 tablespoon (15 ml) flour

1 package frozen puff pastry sheets, thawed in refrigerator

vegetable oil cooking spray

½ cup (120 ml) margarine

¼ cup (60 ml) honey

Steps

1. Preheat oven to 375° F (190°C.).

2. Place the almonds on a cookie sheet.

3. Toast the almonds in the oven for 4 to 7 minutes or until light golden brown. *Keep an eye on the almonds at all times to make sure they do not overcook!*

4. Using oven mitts, remove the cookie sheet.

5. While the almonds cool, sprinkle the flour on a cutting board. With a rolling pin, gently roll out a pastry sheet until it is smooth.

6. With a knife, cut the sheet into nine equal pieces, as illustrated.

7. Dip a pastry brush in water and wet the top surface of each piece of pastry.

8. Fold the bottom left-hand corner of each piece toward the middle of the piece and press the corner down firmly.

9. Fold the top right-hand corner toward the middle of the piece and press the corner down firmly.

Time
1 hour

Tools
2 cookie sheets

oven mitts

cutting board

rolling pin

knife

pastry brush

small frying pan

spatula

Makes
12 servings

10. Spray the second cookie sheet with vegetable oil cooking spray. Put the pastries on the cookie sheet.

11. Using a knife on a cutting board, chop the almonds. Set aside.

12. Put the margarine in a small frying pan and heat on medium for 2 minutes or until melted.

13. Add the honey. Stir well and cook for 1 minute.

14. Using a pastry brush, brush the margarine and honey mixture on the pastries.

15. Sprinkle the pastries with chopped almonds.

16. Bake the pastries in two batches for 15 to 20 minutes per batch or until golden brown.

17. Using oven mitts, remove the cookie sheet from the oven. Remove pastries with a spatula.

Time
30 minutes

Tools
knife

cutting board

heavy skillet

Makes
4 servings

The term couscous *refers to the finished
dish as well as to the type of wheat flour
that is cooked as an accompaniment
to the stew of lamb or chicken and
vegetables. To make things easier, this
recipe uses packaged instant couscous.*

Ingredients

1   package instant couscous

2   green zucchini

½   head cabbage

1   red pepper

½   pound (227 g) green beans

2   tablespoons (30 ml)
    vegetable oil

½   cup (120 ml) chicken,
    cooked and cut into bite-
    sized pieces

½   cup (120 ml) chicken broth

1   teaspoon (5 ml) saffron

½   teaspoon (3 ml) cardamom

¼   teaspoon (1 ml) ground
    ginger

¼   teaspoon (1 ml) allspice

¼   teaspoon (1 ml) nutmeg

Steps

1. Prepare the couscous according to the package directions. While the couscous cooks, continue with the
following steps.

2. Wash the zucchini, cabbage, red pepper, and green
beans.

3. Using a knife on a cutting board, cut off the ends of
the zucchini and the green beans. Cut the zucchini into
¼-inch (6-mm) slices. Cut the green beans into ½-inch
(12-mm) pieces.

4. Cut the red pepper in half. Remove and discard the
seeds and ribs. Cut the pepper into strips.

5. Cut the cabbage into thin slices.

6. In a heavy skillet, heat the oil over medium-high heat for 2 minutes.
7. Sauté the vegetables in the oil for 6 to 10 minutes or until all vegetables are tender crisp.
8. Add the chicken, broth, and all the spices and bring to a boil.
9. Simmer for 5 minutes.
10. Serve immediately on top of couscous.

CHAPTER 14

GHANA

Ghana is in the middle of west Africa, where grains, such as rice, maize, and millet are staples. **Maize** is actually Native American corn introduced to Africa from North America. Millet comes in many types, varying in size and color. Usually, **millet** is a round, yellow grain that cooks into a fluffy hot cereal.

In home gardens, Ghanaians grow vegetables such as yams and chili peppers. Yams are often confused with sweet potatoes, but real yams are white on the inside and have a rough skin. Yams are served on holidays and special occasions in west Africa. Other popular vegetables are corn, cabbage, and tender greens. West African food is fiery hot, flavored with such seasonings as chili peppers, garlic, and ginger.

Because Ghana borders the Atlantic Ocean, much fish is available. Popular fish includes sardines, tuna, and mackerel. Inland in Ghana there are fish farms, making fish available there as well.

Some west Africans eat three meals a day, but many eat only twice a day. The first meal is eaten late in the morning; the second meal, in the evening. A snack of bread, fried plantains, or fruit may be eaten between meals.

Meals are often made up of bread, rice, millet, or other grains, served with a soup or stew. The soup or stew contains vegetables and, sometimes, small pieces of meat, poultry, or fish. In Ghana, bean stew is popular. It is made of black-eyed peas or black beans, to which dried fish, onions, tomatoes, and other vegetables are added. This stew is commonly eaten with yeast bread and rice, yams, or fried plantains. Desserts, when served, are cooling, such as fruit salad or vanilla custard.

EXPERIMENT

WHAT MAKES PEANUT BUTTER SMOOTH?

Purpose

To learn about the chemical process of hydrogenation.

Materials

1 jar natural peanut butter
1 jar brand-name creamy peanut butter
1 spoon
2 small bowls

Procedure

1. Open both jars of peanut butter.

2. Put two large spoonfuls of the natural peanut butter in one of the bowls. Mix well with the spoon.

3. Put two large spoonfuls of the brand-name creamy peanut butter in the other bowl. Mix well with the spoon.

4. Leave the bowls undisturbed for 1 hour.

5. Carefully examine each dish of peanut butter. Which one is still creamy and smooth in texture? Which one has oil on top of the peanut butter?

What Happened?

The brand-name peanut butter is still creamy and smooth, but the natural peanut butter has a layer of oil on top. Peanuts naturally contain oil. When peanuts are mashed together to make peanut butter, this oil separates from the rest of the peanuts. This is exactly how natural peanut butter looks—it has a layer of oil on top of it. You probably noticed this when you opened the jar. However, most brand-name peanut butter is put through a chemical process called hydrogenation, which gets rid of the oil separation problem.

Hydrogenation is a chemical reaction that turns liquid oil into solid fat by combining the oil with hydrogen gas. The process of hydrogenation actually changes the atoms of the oil to make it a solid rather than a liquid. In addition to making peanut butter a smooth creamy spread, hydrogenation is used to make spreadable margarine from liquid vegetable oils such as corn or sunflower oil.

Use either type of peanut butter to make West African Peanut Soup. Serve it with Spicy Vegetable Stew, Cabbage Salad, and Baked Plantains for a Ghanian meal.

West African Peanut Soup

Time
50 to 60 minutes

Tools
knife

cutting board

large saucepan

Makes
6 servings

Peanuts, called groundnuts in Africa, were introduced to west Africa from Brazil in the sixteenth century. If you like peanuts and peanut butter, you will enjoy this soup!

Ingredients

4 scallions
1 medium carrot
2 stalks celery
1 clove garlic
3 tablespoons (45 ml) margarine
1½ teaspoons (8 ml) curry powder
2 tablespoons (30 ml) all-purpose flour

4 cups (1 L) chicken or vegetable broth
½ cup (120 ml) peanut butter
2 tablespoons (30 ml) ketchup
1 teaspoon (5 ml) soy sauce
2 teaspoons (10 ml) Worcestershire sauce
1 cup (240 ml) rice, cooked

Steps

1. Wash the scallions, carrot, and celery.

2. Using a knife on a cutting board, cut the green tops and root ends off the scallions. Mince the white part.

3. Slice the carrot and celery, then dice.

4. Peel and mince the garlic.

5. Put the margarine in a large saucepan and heat on medium for 2 minutes or until melted.

6. Sauté the scallions, carrots, celery, and garlic in the margarine for 8 to 10 minutes, stirring frequently.

7. Stir in the curry powder and flour. Cook for about 1 minute.

8. Slowly add the broth. Reduce the heat to low and simmer for 20 minutes.

• • • • •
The flour is used to thicken the soup.
• • • • •

9. Stir in the peanut butter, ketchup, soy sauce, and Worcestershire sauce until the soup is smooth.

10. Add the rice and simmer for about 10 minutes.

11. Serve hot in bowls.

Spicy Vegetable Stew

Time
50 minutes

Tools
knife

cutting board

peeler

large saucepan

Makes
4 servings

This stew is one of many stews made in west Africa. To eat this stew as they do in Africa, take a small piece of pita bread and scoop up bits of stew.

Ingredients

1 medium onion

2 cloves garlic

½ pound (227 g) carrots

1 medium potato

½ pound (227 g) green beans

2 tablespoons (30 ml) margarine

1 teaspoon (5 ml) ground red pepper

1 tablespoon (15 ml) paprika

2 medium tomatoes

¼ cup (60 ml) tomato paste

2 cups (480 ml) low-sodium chicken broth

salt and pepper to taste

4 pita pockets

1 cup (240 ml) nonfat or low-fat plain yogurt

Steps

1. Remove the outer, papery skin of the onion.

2. Using a knife on a cutting board, cut the onion in half. Lay each onion half flat on the cutting board and chop.

3. Peel and mince the garlic.

4. Wash and peel the carrots and potato.

5. Slice the carrots, then chop.

6. Cut the potatoes in half, then cut into ½-inch (13-mm) cubes.

7. Wash the green beans and cut into thirds.

8. Put the margarine in a large saucepan and heat on medium for 2 minutes or until melted.

9. Add the onions, garlic, carrots, potatoes, and green beans, along with the red pepper and paprika. Sauté the vegetables for 15 minutes, stirring frequently.

10. While the vegetables are sautéing, wash and chop the tomatoes. Discard the seeds.

11. Add the chopped tomatoes, tomato paste, and chicken broth to the sautéed vegetables. Stir.

12. Set the heat to high until the mixture boils. Then reduce the heat to low and simmer for 15 minutes or until the vegetables are tender when pricked with a fork.

13. Taste the stew and add salt or pepper if needed.

14. Serve the stew in bowls with pita bread and ¼ cup (60 ml) plain yogurt on the side.

Cabbage Salad

Time
30 minutes
plus
1 hour chilling time

Tools
knife

cutting board

colander

large bowl

peeler

grater

small bowl

wire whip

Makes
6 servings

This salad is often served with stew.
The dressing is easy to make: just squeeze
an orange and a lemon and add vegetable oil.

Ingredients

1 head cabbage

3 medium carrots

1 cup (240 ml) pineapple chunks, drained

1 lemon

1 orange

¼ cup (60 ml) vegetable oil

Steps

1. Remove the outer leaves of the cabbage.

2. Using a knife on a cutting board, cut the cabbage into quarters. Remove the core.

3. Rinse the cabbage in a colander under cold running water. Let the water drain out.

4. Thinly slice the cabbage on a cutting board until you have 4 cups (1 L). Place the cabbage in a large bowl.

5. Peel the carrots with a peeler. Cut off the tops and bottoms.

6. Using the largest holes on a grater, shred the carrots until you have 1 cup (240 ml).

7. Put the carrots and pineapple chunks in the large bowl with the cabbage.

8. Using a knife on a cutting board, cut the lemon and orange in half. Squeeze the juice of both into a small bowl.

9. Make a salad dressing by whisking the vegetable oil into the juice.

10. Pour the salad dressing over the cabbage and toss well.

11. Refrigerate for at least 1 hour before serving.

Baked Plantains

Plantains are a tropical fruit related to bananas. But, unlike bananas, plantains can't be eaten without being cooked first! Green or yellow-green plantains are not as sweet as the deep yellow or brown plantains. Green plantains are often served as a vegetable. Deep yellow and brown plantains are usually served as dessert.

Ingredients

4 deep yellow or brown plantains

4 tablespoons (60 ml) margarine

½ cup (120 ml) brown sugar

½ teaspoon (3 ml) cinnamon

½ teaspoon (3 ml) nutmeg

Time
10 minutes to prepare
plus
35 minutes to bake

Tools
knife

cutting board

baking dish

small frying pan

aluminum foil

Makes
4 servings

Steps

1. Preheat oven to 350°F (175°C).

2. Wash plantains. *Do not peel!* The peels help the fruit keep their shape during baking.

3. Using a knife on a cutting board, cut the plantains in half lengthwise.

4. Put the plantains in a baking dish.

5. Put the margarine in a small frying pan and heat on medium for 2 minutes or until melted.

6. Add the brown sugar, cinnamon, and nutmeg. Stir well and cook for 1 minute.

7. Pour the melted margarine mixture over the plantains. Cover the baking pan with aluminum foil.

8. Bake the plantains for 35 minutes or until tender when pierced with a fork.

NUTRITION IN A NUTSHELL

Nutrition is the science about you and food. It explores the food you eat and how the body uses it. You need food to get energy to play, to breathe, and to keep your heart beating. The energy in food is called **calories.** Food also provides a variety of substances called **nutrients** that your body needs to grow, to repair itself, and to stay healthy.

A booklet from the U.S. Department of Agriculture and the U.S. Department for Health and Human Services called *Dietary Guidelines for Americans* provides the following answers to the question "What should we be eating to stay healthy?"

1. *Eat a variety of foods.* You need more than 40 different nutrients for good health.

2. *Maintain a healthy weight.* If you are too fat or too thin, your chances of developing health problems are increased. To lose weight, you need to eat fewer calories (calories tell us how much energy is packed in each food).

3. *Choose a diet low in fat and cholesterol.* **Fat** is a nutrient that supplies more energy than any other nutrient. People who eat diets high in fat are more likely to have heart disease and certain types of cancer than people who don't. Some fats you eat you can actually see—such as margarine, vegetable oil, and butter. But many other fats are not so obvious—such as the fat in hamburgers, in whole milk and many cheeses, in cookies, cakes, fried foods, mayonnaise, salad dressings, and other foods. **Cholesterol** is a fatlike nutrient made in the body and found in every cell. Eggs and liver contain the highest amounts of cholesterol found in foods.

4. *Eat plenty of vegetables, fruits, and grain products, such as breads, cereals, pasta, and rice.* These foods are generally low in fats. By choosing them often, you are likely to decrease fats and increase carbohydrates in your diet. **Carbohydrates**

are a group of nutrients that include sugar, starch, and fiber. **Fiber** is found only in plant foods such as fruits, vegetables, and grains. Eating fiber has many desirable effects.

5. *Don't use a lot of sugar.* Sugars and foods that contain them in large amounts supply calories but few nutrients. Therefore, people don't need much sugar and it can add unnecessary weight.

6. *Don't use a lot of salt and sodium.* Table salt contains sodium and chlorine—two minerals needed in your diet. However, most Americans eat more salt and sodium than they need. Sodium is also added to a lot of foods during processing. Always check labels carefully before you buy.

THE FOOD GUIDE PYRAMID

Another way to look at what we need to eat each day is pictured in the accompanying illustration, the Food Guide Pyramid. The Food Guide Pyramid emphasizes foods from the five food groups shown in the three lower sections. Each of these food groups provides some, but not all, of the nutrients you need. Foods in one group can't replace those in another. No one food group is more important than another—for good health, you need them all. But you need more of some groups, such as bread, than others, such as fats. Also, vary your choices of foods within each group, because specific foods differ in the kinds and amounts of nutrients they provide.

The Food Guide Pyramid
A Guide to Daily Food Choices

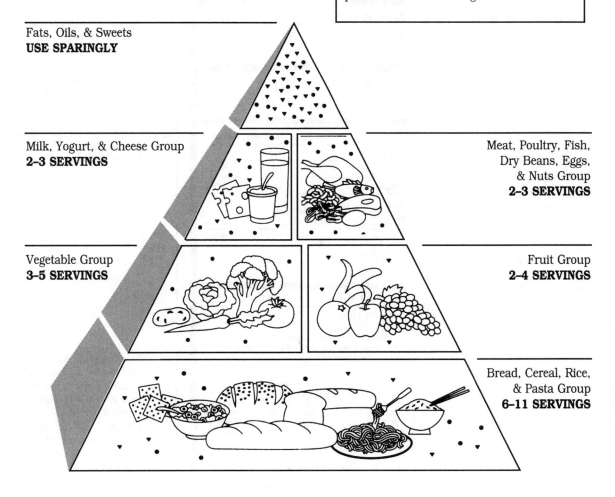

Fats, Oils, & Sweets
USE SPARINGLY

Milk, Yogurt, & Cheese Group
2–3 SERVINGS

Meat, Poultry, Fish,
Dry Beans, Eggs,
& Nuts Group
2–3 SERVINGS

Vegetable Group
3–5 SERVINGS

Fruit Group
2–4 SERVINGS

Bread, Cereal, Rice,
& Pasta Group
6–11 SERVINGS

HOW TO READ A FOOD LABEL

Have you ever noticed that little section of the food label called Nutrition Facts on the foods you buy at the supermarket? Let's check it out—from top to bottom—on a frozen dinner.

The serving size is 12 ounces—that's ¾ pound. This package has 1 serving in it, so you'd have to eat all the food in the package to get the amounts of the nutrients listed.

There are 340 calories in the serving, and 45 of those calories come from fat. That doesn't seem bad at all.

The nutrients listed are those most important to the health of the average American. You should try to eat 100% of your carbohydrate, fiber, vitamin, and mineral values in one day, over several meals. You should keep down the percentage of fat, saturated fat, cholesterol, and sodium. This food is not too high in fat and cholesterol and is a good source of fiber, protein, and vitamin C.

The % Daily Value column tells you how much of the daily recommended amount of a nutrient this food contributes to a 2,000-calorie diet. Your daily values may be higher or lower depending on how many calories you need.

At the bottom of the label are listed the recommended amounts of various nutrients for a 2,000- and a 2,500-calorie diet. For fat, cholesterol, and sodium, the amounts are maximums— you should try to eat *less* than the listed amounts.

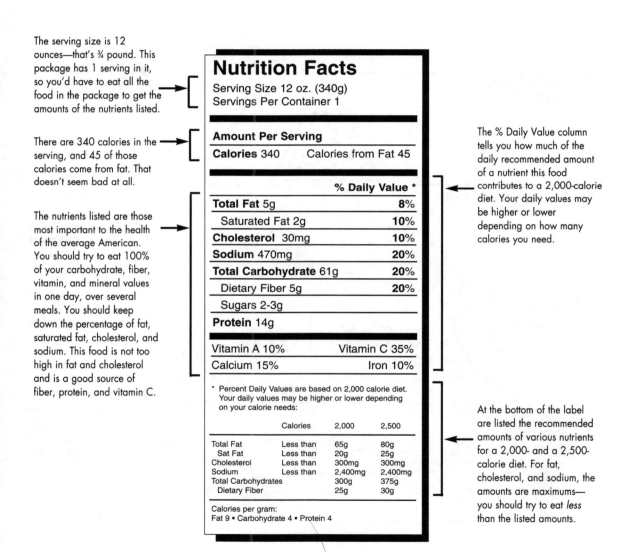

Nutrition Facts

Serving Size 12 oz. (340g)
Servings Per Container 1

Amount Per Serving

Calories 340   Calories from Fat 45

	% Daily Value *
Total Fat 5g	8%
Saturated Fat 2g	10%
Cholesterol 30mg	10%
Sodium 470mg	20%
Total Carbohydrate 61g	20%
Dietary Fiber 5g	20%
Sugars 2-3g	
Protein 14g	

Vitamin A 10%	Vitamin C 35%
Calcium 15%	Iron 10%

* Percent Daily Values are based on 2,000 calorie diet. Your daily values may be higher or lower depending on your calorie needs:

	Calories	2,000	2,500
Total Fat	Less than	65g	80g
Sat Fat	Less than	20g	25g
Cholesterol	Less than	300mg	300mg
Sodium	Less than	2,400mg	2,400mg
Total Carbohydrates		300g	375g
Dietary Fiber		25g	30g

Calories per gram:
Fat 9 • Carbohydrate 4 • Protein 4

B
NUTRIENT CONTENT OF RECIPES

This table shows the amount of calories, fat, cholesterol, fiber, and sodium contained in one serving of each recipe in this book. You can compare these numbers to how much you need daily.

Recipe	Serving Size	Calories	Fat (grams)	Cholesterol (milligrams)	Fiber (grams)	Sodium (milligrams)
Chapter 1. CANADA						
Southwestern Ontario Fruit Salad	¾ cup (170 g)	89	3	0	30	2
Open-Faced Barbecue Beef Sandwich	1 sandwich	640	17	69	4	1212
Maple Syrup Baked Beans	½ cup (113 g)	189	1	0	9	544
Chapter 2. MEXICO						
Mexican Bean Salad	½ cup (113 g)	136	4	0	4	471
Sizzling Chicken Fajitas	1 fajita	246	7	51	2	421
Confetti Rice	½ cup (113 g)	116	2	0	1	275
Fast 'n' Easy Cornbread	1 piece	219	8	47	2	261
Rice Pudding	½ cup (113 g)	151	2	31	1	40
Chapter 3. BRAZIL						
Iced Coffee and Chocolate Float	1 serving	187	8	34	0	95
Mocha-Flavored Cupcakes	1 cupcake	252	11	19	0	158
Best Beef Kabobs	1 kabob	297	9	72	2	387
Fruited Rice	¾ cup (170 g)	236	3	0	2	36

Recipe	Serving Size	Calories	Fat (grams)	Cholesterol (milligrams)	Fiber (grams)	Sodium (milligrams)
Chapter 4. ITALY						
Focaccia with Sun-Dried Tomatoes	1 serving	271	13	11	1	386
Antipasto Salad	1 serving	275	22	48	2	699
Cannoli	1 cannoli	294	15	40	1	360
Chapter 5. FRANCE						
Mixed Greens and Celery Salad	1 serving	56	5	0	1	81
Pick-a-Filling Quiche	1 serving	442	28	154	1	335
Dessert Crêpes with Raspberry Sauce	2 crêpes	396	18	76	2	144
Chapter 6. GERMANY						
Sweet-and-Sour Red Cabbage	½ cup (113 g)	73	3	5	0	107
Traditional German Sauerbraten	1 serving	327	14	87	1	507
Spice Cookies	1 cookie	66	4	4	0	26
Chapter 7. SPAIN						
Flan	1 serving	162	6	111	0	54
One-Pot Paella	1 serving	476	16	107	4	542
Pimiento Drop Biscuits	1 biscuit	112	4	1	1	229
Chapter 8. ISRAEL						
Potato Pancakes	1 pancake	193	6	142	1	246
Cheese Blintzes	1 blintz	166	10	67	1	278
Lemony Coconut Cookies	1 cookie	107	3	44	1	37

Recipe	Serving Size	Calories	Fat (grams)	Cholesterol (milligrams)	Fiber (grams)	Sodium (milligrams)
Chapter 9. INDIA						
Carrots with Grated Coconut and Raisins	½ cup (113 g)	143	5	0	3	83
Lentil and Noodle Soup	¾ cup (170 g)	268	6	13	0	727
Baked Fish Topped with Coconut-Tomato Chutney	1 serving	374	20	62	3	680
Chapatis	1 chapati	62	0	0	2	153
Mango with Yogurt Dressing	1 serving	93	3	3	2	41
Chapter 10. CHINA						
Bubbly Mandarin Orange–Pineapple Flaat	1 serving	405	10	40	0	133
Chopstick-Friendly Chicken and Veggie Stir-Fry	1 serving	299	7	56	2	590
Awesome Egg Rolls	1 egg roll	339	16	105	1	321
Incredible Almond Cookies	1 cookie	161	9	38	1	125
Chapter 11. JAPAN						
Steamed Broccoli with Sesame Seed Dressing	½ cup (113 g)	56	2	0	2	528
Fast 'n' Easy Beef Teriyaki	3 oz. (85 g)	203	8	81	0	318
Japanese Soba Noodles in Broth	1 serving	90	1	1	0	435

Recipe	Serving Size	Calories	Fat (grams)	Cholesterol (milligrams)	Fiber (grams)	Sodium (milligrams)
Chapter 12. THAILAND						
Thai Salad with Bean Sprouts	1 serving	89	5	0	2	33
Zippy Fried Rice with Chicken	1 serving	518	13	50	4	998
Banana-Nut Dessert	1 serving	201	5	9	0	240
Chapter 13. MOROCCO						
Almond and Honey Pastries	1 pastry	182	13	0	0	105
Couscous	1 serving	236	9	16	7	231
Chapter 14. GHANA						
West African Peanut Soup	1 cup (227 g)	259	17	1	2	844
Spicy Vegetable Stew	1 serving	320	9	4	4	901
Cabbage Salad	1 serving	142	9	0	3	20
Baked Plantains	1 serving	422	12	0	0	168

C WHAT'S SAFE TO EAT?

Even if you choose a very nutritious diet, there are still dangers lurking in your food. They seem to be reported on television and in the newspapers and magazines all the time. Are apples really sprayed with a dangerous chemical? Is eating an undercooked fast-food hamburger going to hospitalize you? Let's look at how to keep food safe.

FOOD POISONING

Foodborne illness, commonly called food poisoning, is caused by substances in food such as bacteria and molds, which make you sick to your stomach but can be even more serious. Sometimes fever and infection occur. The symptoms may start within an hour of eating the suspected food or up to several days later.

Foodborne illness is most often caused by microorganisms. Microorganisms include bacteria and viruses. *Micro* means "small," and both bacteria and viruses are so small that they cannot be seen by the naked eye. Bacteria are in the air, in the ground, and on you and me. Given the right temperature and enough time, bacteria will multiply in food (they double in number every 20 minutes). Bacteria cause foodborne illness when they multiply in food to the point that, when the food is eaten, they make you very sick. Luckily, not all bacteria cause foodborne illness; only a small number do.

Bacteria grow readily under these three conditions.

1. **In a food that contains some protein,** such as meat, poultry, fish, eggs, dairy products, gravies and sauces, potatoes, beans, and rice.

2. **At a temperature between 40°F (4°C) and 140°F (60°C).** Refrigeration is normally at or below 45° F (7°C), so bacteria grow slowly if at all. Bacterial growth slows down even more in the freezer, which is usually kept at or below 0°F (−18°C). Room temperature is normally around 70°F (21°C)—a great temperature for bacteria to grow.

3. For at least 2 hours in the temperature zone given in condition 2.

In some, but not all, cases, adequate cooking of the contaminated food (to 165°F or 74°C) will prevent problems. However, cooking does not kill all forms of bacteria, and in many cases the contaminated food may not even be cooked further, as in the case of tuna salad.

Here are some ways to prevent foodborne illness in your home.

1. Keep hot foods hot and cold foods cold (below 40°F or 4°C).

2. Wash your hands frequently, especially after handling raw meat, poultry, seafood, or eggs.

3. Don't touch yourself while handling food, because bacteria on your skin can then be introduced into the food. Don't use your fingers to taste food—use a spoon.

4. Cover all cuts, burns, and boils with a waterproof bandage. Cuts, burns, and boils are the home to many bacteria that you don't want in your food.

5. Keep all equipment sparkling clean and wash after every use. For instance, if you use your cutting board for cutting chicken, wash it thoroughly with *hot* water and soap before cutting lettuce on it (wash your knife, too)!

6. Use a different spoon for stirring raw foods, such as meat that is being browned, and cooked foods.

7. Cook and reheat foods until they are very hot and well done.

8. Don't eat raw meat, fish, or eggs. They may contain harmful bacteria, viruses, or parasites. If a dough or batter contains raw eggs, don't eat it before it is cooked!

9. Thaw meats, poultry, and seafood in the refrigerator overnight. Don't leave them out to thaw.

These are good rules to follow. A final rule of thumb is: "When in doubt, throw it out." It's probably not worth getting sick about.

MOLDS

Ever notice a little bluish green fuzz growing on your tomatoes? You probably knew it was just mold but wondered if you could just cut out the moldy spot or if you should throw out the entire tomato. Molds cause spoilage (most often of fruits and bread), musty odors, and yucky flavors in foods. Molds also grow on vegetables, meats, and cheese that have been exposed to the air. Although molds will be killed by most cooking, the toxins (poisons) they produce will not, so you need to avoid eating moldy food. In foods with a firm texture, such as potatoes and hard cheeses, you can just cut out the moldy area. When dealing with a soft food, such as bread or tomatoes, it is best to throw the food out if you find any mold on it.

To avoid a dangerous mold that grows on peanuts (and corn), it is best to buy national brands. Also, throw out any moldy peanuts, peanut butter, cornmeal, or other corn products.

PESTICIDES

Pesticides are chemicals used to control insects, diseases, weeds, fungi, mold, and other pests on plants, vegetables, fruits, and animals. Pesticides are normally applied to crops as a spray, fog, or dust.

The government allows a small amount of pesticides to be left on the food you buy, but to be safe, you should avoid eating them. Here's how.

- Buy organically grown fruits and vegetables (these are grown without the use of pesticides) when possible.
- Throw away the outer leaves of leafy vegetables such as lettuce.
- Wash fruits and vegetables carefully, using a brush.
- Peel carrots, waxed cucumbers, peaches, and pears, because these foods are more likely to have hazardous pesticide residues.
- Buy local produce, as it is probably treated with less pesticide than produce that has to travel a long distance.
- Trim fat and skin from meat, poultry, and fish. Pesticides in animal feed can concentrate in animal fat. Skim fat from pan drippings, broths, sauces, and soups.
- Eat a varied diet so that no one food dominates.

GLOSSARY

abendbrot The German word for supper.

acid A group of chemicals that taste sour, neutralize bases, and turn purple cabbage juice red.

antipasto (plural **antipasti**) Italian appetizer.

atmospheric (or **air**) **pressure** The force that billions of molecules of air exert as they speed around.

b'stilla An African dish made of dough stuffed with layers of pigeon meat, spices, and sugar, and then fried.

baguette A long, thin loaf of French bread.

barometer A device that measures air pressure.

base A group of chemicals that taste bitter, neutralize acids, and turn purple cabbage juice green.

beat To move a utensil back and forth to blend ingredients together.

bicarbonate of soda Also called baking soda, a basic substance.

blintz A thin pancake filled with a cheese mixture and browned in a frying pan. A popular dish in Israel.

boeuf bourguignon A French beef stew made with burgundy wine.

boil To cook at the boiling point of water: 212°F (100°C).

bok choy Another name for Chinese cabbage, a vegetable with long white stalks and green leaves.

bouillabaisse A fish stew made with olive oil, garlic, and tomatoes made in Provence, France.

braten The German name for roasted meat.

cafe con leche The Spanish name for coffee with milk

calamares The Spanish word for squid.

calorie A measure of the energy in food.

Camembert A type of cheese made in Normandy, France.

cannoli An Italian dessert consisting of little pipes of sweet pastry dough filled with ricotta cheese, pudding, or whipped cream.

carbohydrate A group of nutrients that include sugar, starch, and fiber and that provide the body with energy.

carbon dioxide A gas that is used to make soft drinks fizzy.

cassava (or **manioc**) A starchy root eaten in Brazil and other countries.

cassoulet A rich stew made with goose or duck, pork or mutton, plus sausage and white beans in Languedoc, France.

cell The smallest unit of a living thing.

chapati A round flatbread of India that is made of whole wheat flour.

chemical indicator A substance that turns colors to indicate the presence of certain substances.

chemical reaction The breaking apart of substances to make new substances.

chlorophyll The green pigment of plants.

cholesterol A fatlike nutrient made in the body and found in every cell.

chop To cut into irregularly shaped pieces.

chorizo A spicy red sausage made in western Spain.

chutney An Indian relish made from fruits, vegetables, and herbs.

cilantro Leaves of the herb coriander which has a strong, distinctive flavor.

cocido A rich Spanish dish of boiled beef.

coq au vin A French chicken casserole made with burgundy wine.

coriander An Old World herb of the carrot family.

couscous A northern African dish made with a type of wheat flour that is steamed over a stew of lamb or chicken and vegetables.

cream To mix a fat (usually margarine or butter) and sugar by pressing them against a bowl with the back of a spoon until they look creamy.

crêpe Thin pancake made in France.

criouch A Moroccan cake covered with honey and sesame seeds.

croissant A flaky, crescent-shaped roll made in France.

cut in To combine a fat with flour using a cutting motion until the mixture is in the shape of peas.

daikon A giant white radish grown in Japan.

dehydrate To remove moisture or water.

density The mass of an object per unit of volume.

dice To cut into cubes of the same size.

Dijon mustard A spicy type of mustard from Dijon, France.

dim sum A Chinese dish consisting of steamed dumplings stuffed with meat or seafood.

dulse A sun-dried red seaweed eaten as a snack in the Canadian province of New Brunswick.

egg roll A Chinese wheat dough that is filled with meat and vegetables, then fried.

egg wash A mixture of egg and water that can be brushed on foods to make them shine after being baked or to help them hold together.

embryo The seed from which a new plant will grow.

empanada A thick Spanish seafood or meat pie that is often served cold.

fajita A tortilla wrapped around pieces of grilled meat or poultry and vegetables. A popular dish in Mexico.

fat A nutrient that supplies more energy than any other nutrient.

feijoada A popular dish in Brazil made of beef, black beans, sausage, and usually, rice.

felafel An ancient dish of the Arabian peninsula that is made of pita bread filled with mashed chickpeas and cracked wheat.

fiber A carbohydrate found only in plant foods such as fruits, vegetables, and grains.

finocchio The Italian name for a green vegetable called fennel in English.

flan The Spanish name for caramel custard.

focaccia An Italian flatbread like the crust of a deep-dish pizza that is topped with sun-dried tomatoes, onions, olives, herbs, and cheese.

fold To mix ingredients using a gentle over-and-under motion with a utensil.

gazpacho A cold Spanish soup made of tomatoes, green peppers, cucumber, and garlic.

gel A baked custard, so called because it has gelled, or become solid.

gelatinization The process by which starches absorb water and double in size.

gelato The Italian word for ice cream.

gluten An elastic substance in flour that gives bread its sturdy texture.

goulash A highly seasoned Hungarian stew of beef, veal, or pork made with onions, potatoes, tomatoes, peppers, and dumplings.

grate To rub a food across a grater's tiny punched holes to produce small or fine pieces of food.

grissini Golden sticks of bread made in the Piedmont region of Italy.

guacamole A Mexican dip made from mashed avocado.

hilum The point where the dry bean is attached to the pod and where water is absorbed into the bean.

hoisin sauce A dark, sweet Chinese sauce made from soybeans, sugar, and spices.

hydrogenation A chemical reaction that combines a substance with hydrogen gas; in particular, the reaction that turns liquid oil into solid fat.

kabobs Small pieces of raw meat, poultry, or seafood, placed with vegetables onto a skewer and broiled.

kaffee The German word for an afternoon snack.

kneading The process of working dough into a smooth mass by pressing and folding.

kumquat A small fruit that resembles an orange but is not citrus fruit.

latke The Israeli name for potato pancake.

litchi A round, red fruit with a raisinlike flavor.

maize Native American corn.

mango An oval or round fruit weighing from 1 to 5 pounds that Indians have grown for thousands of years.

marinade A sauce in which meat is soaked to soften and flavor it.

marinate To soak in marinade.

matzo meal Finely ground matzo, a flat unleavened bread eaten during the Jewish holiday of Passover

millet A round, yellow grain that cooks into a fluffy hot cereal.

mince To chop very fine.

miso Soybean paste.

misoshiru A Japanese soup made with miso, tofu, seaweed, and vegetables.

mix To combine ingredients so that they are evenly distributed.

mocha The flavor that results from blending coffee and chocolate or cocoa.

molecule A very small particle of matter.

molinillo A wooden beater used in Mexico to whip a hot chocolate drink into a froth.

mortadella A spicy Italian sausage with cubes of animal fat and black peppercorns.

nam pla prig A Thai sauce made from fish sauce, garlic, red peppers, and lemon juice.

naan An Indian flatbread that uses yeast to make it rise a little.

neutral Neither acid nor base.

nori A type of Japanese seaweed that is dried in sheets and crumbled over rice.

nutrient One of many substances in food that are needed for the body to grow, to repair itself, and to stay healthy.

nutrition The science that explores the food we eat and how the body uses it.

okra A long, green vegetable with edible seeds.

osmosis The process by which water flows across a plant's cell wall to enter the plant cell.

paella A Spanish rice stew made with chicken, shellfish, and vegetables.

paneer A kind of cottage cheese made in India.

panfry To cook in a pan over moderate heat in a small amount of fat.

plantain A tropical fruit related to bananas that must be cooked before eating.

polenta Cornmeal mush, popular in Italy.

proscuitto A spicy Italian ham.

quiche A French egg and cream tart typically filled with cheese, spinach, mushrooms, ham, or other vegetables and meat.

raita A mixture of grated vegetables and yogurt popular in India.

rambutan A red, oval-shaped fruit native to Thailand.

ras al hanout A Moroccan spice mixture consisting of cinnamon, cumin, coriander, ginger, and turmeric.

rice wine vinegar A vinegar made from rice wine that is used as a seasoning in Japan.

risotto A creamy rice dish to which many different ingredients can be added. Popular in Italy.

salsa A Mexican sauce made from tomatoes, onion, chili peppers, garlic, and other ingredients.

samosa A deep-fried turnover stuffed with meat, potatoes, or vegetables. Popular in India.

sauerbraten A traditional German dish made from bottom round or other beef roast.

sauerkraut A German dish made from fermented cabbage.

sauté To cook quickly in a pan over medium-high heat in a small amount of fat.

seed coat The hard outer skin of dry beans.

shaddock A fruit similar to grapefruit that is native to Thailand.

shoyu Japanese soy sauce.

shred To rub a food across a surface with medium to large holes or slits to produce small pieces of food.

siesta The period from 2 to 4 P.M. in Spain when businesses and schools close down so that families can have dinner together.

simmer To cook in a liquid that is just below the boiling point.

slice To cut into uniform slices.

soba noodles Flat, thin, brownish gray, Japanese noodles made from buckwheat flour.

sol Stirred custard.

spaetzle A German dumpling made from wheat flour.

specific gravity A comparison of the density of an object to the density of water.

starches A form of carbohydrate, the nutrient that provides the body with energy.

steam To cook in steam.

stir-fry To cook bite-sized pieces of food over medium-high heat in a small amount of oil while stirring constantly.

stollen A German fruit bread.

tandoor A clay oven used in India.

tandoori An Indian meat or chicken dish that is first marinated with oil and spices and then roasted on skewers.

tempura A Japanese dish consisting of food coated with batter and deep-fried.

teriyaki A Japanese process of cooking, by which meat or seafood is broiled with a sauce.

tofu A cheeselike Chinese food made from soybeans.

tortilla A thin, flat pancake eaten as bread in Mexico.

tortilleria A store in Mexico that sells fresh tortillas.

toss To mix ingredients lightly until they are well coated with a dressing or well blended.

venison Deer meat, a popular game meat in the Yukon territory of Canada.

vinaigrette A French word that means "vinegar dressing," a mixture of vinegar, oil, and seasonings.

viscosity A liquid's resistance to flow.

wasabi A green Japanese radish with a strong flavor.

whip To beat rapidly using a circular motion, usually with a wire whip, to incorporate air into the mixture (such as in making whipped cream).

whisk To beat ingredients together lightly with a wire whip until they are well blended.

Wiener schnitzel Sliced veal that is breaded and fried.

wok An all-purpose Chinese pan that is commonly used for stir-frying.

wurst A German sausage.

yakitori A classic Japanese flavoring that comines soy sauce, rice wine, and sugar.

INDEX

C

Watercress, 116

Weather prediction, 35–36

Weight, 149

West African Peanut Soup, 142–143, 156

Whipping, 9, 165

Whisking, 9, 165

Wiener schnitzel, 82, 165

Wine, 53

Wire rack, 6

Wire whip, 6

Wok, 104, 165

Wooden spoon, 6

Wurst, 62, 165

Yakitori, 117, 165

Yams, 139

Yeast, 49

Yogurt Dressing, 102

Yukon Territory (Canada), 16

Zippy Fried Rice with Chicken, 128–129, 156